The Philippians Mindset

The Philippians Mindset

Christian Poleynard

Behind the Veil Books

Copyright © 2021 Christian D Poleynard

All rights reserved.

No part of this publication may be reproduced, stored in a retrieval system, or transmitted, in any form or by any means, without the prior permission in writing of the publisher, nor be otherwise circulated in any form of binding or cover other than that in which it is published and without a similar condition including this condition being imposed on the subsequent purchaser.

Scripture taken from the New King James Version®. Copyright © 1982 by Thomas Nelson. Used by permission. All rights reserved.

Published by Behind the Veil Books

ISBN 978-0-578-34903-9

Cover design by Ayden Poleynard
Cover illustration © 2021 by Ayden Poleynard

Typesetting services by BOOKOW.COM

For Katy, Nathan, Ayden, and Ian

I'm the richest man......

Acknowledgments

Special Thanks to Gillian Coffey and Jason Powell for their reading of the manuscript and their suggestions- a labor of love!

Also, with much appreciation to "Barnabas" Creighton for his constant encouragement.

Scripture taken from the New King James Version®. Copyright © 1982 by Thomas Nelson. Used by permission. All rights reserved.

Contents

Introduction	1
Chapter One	3
Joy	5
Confidence	8
Solidarity	11
Affection	14
Chapter Two	17
Identifying Goodness	21
Being Genuine	24
Chapter Three	31
Assurance of Deliverance	33
To Live is Christ, To Die is Gain	35
Determined To Remain	40
Chapter Four	45
Worthy of the Gospel	46
Together for the Gospel	49
Granted to Suffer for the Gospel	55
Chapter Five	60
The Beauty of Christian Love	61
The Unity of Christian Love	66
The Humility of Christian Love	68
The Humility of Christ's Love	72

Chapter Six	**77**
To Know Christ Personally	79
To Know Christ in Power	82
To know Christ in Suffering	85
Chapter Seven	**91**
Considering Ourselves as Always Wanting	93
Not Considering Anything about Ourselves	98
Only Considering One Thing in Life	101
Chapter Eight	**106**
Rejoice in the Lord	109
Gentle Before the Lord	111
Pray to the Lord	114
Chapter Nine	**120**
Chapter Ten	**133**
Conclusion	**145**
Bibliography	**147**

Introduction

There is something absolutely wonderful that is going on at all times, in every city, town, or wherever you find yourself. It is happening at multiple points in the very place you are reading this book at this very moment. It is especially happening as you read the word of God and think about it. It happens on a Sunday morning as the people of God digest the preaching and express themselves in the truths of the hymns and spiritual songs that are sung during the church service. It happens as Christians commune with one another in the Body of Christ in fellowship, encouragement, and conversation.

This marvelous thing we are talking about is that you, the reader, as well as all peoples on the face of the earth are *perceiving reality* at this very moment. We are all living beings who are conscious of our existence. We are exercising the mysterious ability to freely think and to freely move and to freely look around us and speak and to hear. We are creatures made in the image of God and we have a mind and a consciousness. This is astounding!

Throughout our lifetimes we often become dull to recognizing and relishing in this incredible reality: That we are conscious living beings, existing as souls and minds in time and space. This murkiness comes about because through our *minds* we have embraced sin and its consequences; our minds are riddled with the holes, punctured by the disease of sin. We cannot see eternal realities properly as we were designed to, within our mind's eye.

When the Holy Spirit enlightens our minds and regenerates our souls to apprehend the worthiness of Christ and to fly to Him for salvation, when we are born again and begin to rely on Jesus as our sufficiency for all things, then our minds begin a journey of renewal and recovery. This is a journey which (when death takes the saint into glory) eventually brings us into a full conformity with the image of Jesus Christ. During this journey, we must take the means of grace God has given us and seek to order our minds aright in order to be shaped according to the ways of Christ, according to the counsel of the word of God. We read in Romans 12:2: "And do not be conformed to this world, but be transformed by the renewing of your mind, that you may prove what is that good and acceptable and perfect will of God."

The Scriptures reveal to the mind of the Christian how we are to exercise our senses to discern good and evil. They lay out for us a pattern of how to think, what to meditate on, and how we should consider others in the Body of Christ. The Bible shows us how we should think about our enemies, and primarily what we should consider concerning the work of Christ on our behalf, and the glory of God we are destined to behold for all eternity.

Paul's letter to the Philippians was written while he was under house arrest in Rome, sent to the Philippians by the hand of one of the members of the church in Philippi, Epaphroditus, who had come to minister to Paul in his hour of need. Now Epaphroditus was being sent back to the church by Paul with this letter to encourage them. Paul had different issues and concerns when writing this letter. For instance, there is an overall theme of rejoicing in Christ Jesus that we see springing up throughout the letter.

However, this study of the book of Philippians is going to be engaged in analyzing how Christians are to use their minds according to this epistle of Paul. Embedded within this glorious New Testament book are continual references to *mentally-focused* terms. The prayer of this writer is, that as we hone in on these words and groups of words within their context, we might have our minds submerged in "The Philippians Mindset" and that we would gain a deeper understanding of how to live the Christian life.

Chapter One

Paul and Timothy, bondservants of Jesus Christ, To all the saints in Christ Jesus who are in Philippi, with the bishops and deacons: Grace to you and peace from God our Father and the Lord Jesus Christ. I thank my God upon every remembrance of you, always in every prayer of mine making request for you all with joy, for your fellowship in the gospel from the first day until now, being confident of this very thing, that He who has begun a good work in you will complete it until the day of Jesus Christ: just as it is right for me to think this of you all, because I have you in my heart, inasmuch as both in my chains and in the defense and confirmation of the gospel, you all are partakers with me of grace. For God is my witness, how greatly I long for you all with the affection of Jesus Christ.- Philippians 1:1-8

One of the things I admire about my brother-in-law, Gary, is that he is thoughtful. I am not meaning that he is a deep thinker, necessarily (though I am sure he can be!). What Gary often does is think about other people. Not only does he think about others, but he often considers and ponders what it is that people he cares about like to do, think, and enjoy. My brother-in-law actually writes down notes when he catches someone discussing the things that they are interested in.

Perhaps you also know someone like this. Gary actually carries these notes about the people he loves with him when he travels around for business. If he happens to see something when he is in the marketplace that he knows would bless someone in their area of interest, he will buy it and give it to them later as a gift. You see, Gary spends time considering and recollecting things about other people.

The first mindset we encounter in this book, is that of Paul's own thoughts: specifically, his own consideration of the members of the church in Philippi. In verse 3 we read: "I thank my God upon every 'remembrance' of you." There is our first mental word: *remembrance*. This is the Greek word *mneia* which gives the sense of recollecting in prayer in our passage.

We can see Paul sitting down and smiling as He turns to God in prayer and begins to thank Him as he *recalls* all the good things about his beloved flock in Philippi. We are going to see that Paul first recalls the saints prayerfully with *joy*; secondly with *confidence*; third that he does it with *solidarity*; and finally, that he does it with *affection*.

You see, the first mindset we encounter in Philippians is the mindset contained within Paul's prayers. They are not prayers about a laundry list of things that need to get done, nor are they prayers regarding specific detailed issues in the lives of the church members (though that can be a legitimate subject of prayer). Instead, Paul is praying as a way to recall and bring to remembrance his dear children in Christ. He does this in a way that considers the great position Christ has brought them into, and the graces Christ has purchased for them. Paul is bringing the members of this local church into mindful recollection in such a way that he can thank God for the great gospel realities that are theirs in Christ.

As we consider some of the details of his recollection with joy, confidence, solidarity, and affection, it is important to do so with a mind to emulate Paul in our own prayer lives. Do we have this kind of mindset the book of Philippians begins to pattern for us? Do we have the mindset of Paul in his prayer life: that of recalling our fellow church members before God in prayer as Paul says he did, "always in every prayer of mine"?

Do you want to have joy, confidence, and solidarity with others and affection towards others as part of your regular experience? Would you like to exchange bouts of depression for these qualities of the mind? Do you seek to be useful and live a meaningful life for Jesus Christ? Do you long to impact people's lives for the glory of God? If you have answered yes to these questions then read on and let us look together at how Paul the apostle, our pattern as he followed Christ (1 Tim. 1:16), remembered the saints in Philippi before God in his prayers.

Joy

So first, he did so with joy: verses 3-5:"I thank my God upon every remembrance of you, always in every prayer of mine making request for you all *with joy*- FOR, your fellowship in the gospel from the first day until now" (italics and capitalization mine).

Paul took joy and delight and his soul warmed over with loving happiness when he remembered before God the fact that his dear brothers and sisters in Christ had fellowship with him in the gospel. The word for fellowship is *koinonia*, and in many places means communion or fellowship, but is better translated here as "participation"[1]. Paul was overjoyed that his ministry had born fruit in the Philippians' lives to the point of them bearing their own fruit for the sake of the gospel. They were *participating* in the cause of the gospel. No doubt, we see a pastoral and an apostolic joy and thanksgiving for the Philippians having taken the treasure of the gospel and owned it to the extent of sacrificing and sticking out their necks for the cause of the gospel.

The church in Philippi had sent Paul monetary aid. Ephaphroditus, a member of their congregation, had risked his life to bring this gift to Paul in Rome. They had also been a church which had participated by digging down deep into their own pockets (likely they were not very deep to begin with) and had sent money to help the church in Jerusalem according to Paul's desire for the Gentile churches to support the church where the gospel had been birthed. Furthermore, the Philippians were spreading the good news of Jesus Christ in their local community as well. So it is that Paul had this fatherly kind of joy in the fact that the Philippians were participating in the gospel. He rejoiced as he recalled that his own

---

[1] Moises Silva. *Philippians- Baker Exegetical Commentary on the New Testament* (Baker Academic, 2005), 42

blood, sweat and tears shed in the cause of loving them in the name of Christ had brought about living fruit in their lives.

Interestingly, when we take the word *koinonia* and translate it as "fellowship", as the NKJV does, we still must carry with it the sense of participation in the gospel, but we get with it another angle: Paul rejoiced in having like-minded brothers and sisters whom he could relate to in the sufferings for the cause of the gospel, in the joys of having known the saving grace of Jesus Christ in their lives, and in the bond of love they had for each other. All of them (Paul and the Philippians) knew the joy of being born again so that they could take heart and be encouraged because they all longed to be about their Father's business in spreading the flame of Christianity in the ancient world.

Now this is where *we* come into this passage. Do we think of other Christians in this way? Do we thank God for other believers? Thanking Him that we know the fellowship of the gospel with brothers and sisters in the Lord Jesus Christ? Do we relish in the fact that we are all together as part of a spiritual family; each of us individually plucked from the fires of destruction and a life bent on living as children of wrath and haters of God and as lovers of sin?

Do we come to church on the Lord's day with praise and thankfulness in our hearts to our Father in heaven because we have come amongst those with whom we have fellowship in the gospel with? Do we take time throughout the week to bring those in the body of Christ before God's throne in prayer? Do we thank Him for redeeming our fellow brothers and sisters, and pray for grace in their lives to spread the flame of the gospel throughout their workweek and amongst their family members? Do we encourage each other in our fellowship in the gospel, sharing each other's burdens which are hindering us from living more fully for the cause of Christ, and praying for each other's burdens regarding those we are witnessing to in our families and our workplaces?

Do we find joy in the fellowship of the gospel and in our participation together in the gospel? May we as Christians not lose sight of the reason that brought us into communion and friendship with other believers. It is because of the glorious gospel of Jesus Christ our Savior! Let us look beyond each other's faults and shortcomings and our tendencies to be "uncool" or awkward socially. Let us overlook one another's lack-luster when it comes to being interesting in conversation, perhaps. Let us take joy in one another because we are the church, the bride of Christ. We are fellow soldiers on the battlefield for souls and on the pilgrimage of the Christian life!

Men who fight in combat together many times experience a deep and lasting bond of fellowship and friendship. Because they have held each other's lives in their hands, suffered together, and lived alongside each other in the trenches, there can be an automatic joining of heart and soul amongst these comrades. Those of us who are Christ's have a bond sealed by the blood of Christ, a bond that will see us as companions along the span of all eternity. It is a bond we should relish in *now*, with joy and thankfulness. We should do so with joy that produces the fruit of genuinely caring for each other and taking delight in the good qualities we can find in each member of Christ's body.

The mindset we are to have in the Christian life is that of Paul: of recollecting with joy in prayer to God the like-mindedness we have with the members of the church of Jesus Christ. But it does not simply mean we direct our focus toward our own local church. As we read here in Philippians, Paul was a great distance physically from the Philippians as he recalled the members of that beloved flock. Do we remember our brothers and sisters in other congregations, in other parts of the world, before God with joy?

But what about believers who are not part of our particular denomination? What about churches who do not understand or preach the doctrines of grace as your church perhaps believes? Paul says later in this chapter when speaking of some who preach Christ from envy and strife and some from goodwill: "What then? Only that in every way, whether in pretense or in truth, Christ is preached; and in this I rejoice, yes, and will rejoice." (Phil. 1:18)

Can you take joy in fellowship with a Christian you meet on an airplane who is not a Reformed Christian? Or, if you are an Arminian, can you take joy in fellowship with a Calvinistic Christian? Rather than bristling over with distaste at someone's theological ignorance, we would do better to "meditate on whatever is just and pure and lovely and of good report" (Phil. 4:8) in the lives and the witness of other believers not exactly like us, and learn from their gifts and actually love them. It does not mean we need to have them preach from our pulpits necessarily; but the Body of Christ, by the sovereign providence of God, is much more grand than our denominational or associational world. Do we recall to mind with joy in prayer and thanksgiving all that God is doing through Christians throughout the world? All in all, when we pray for each other, we should do so with the mindset of stirring up a rejoicing spirit in our hearts for the fact that together we have fellowship in the gospel by the grace of God.

Confidence

Secondly, we see Paul recollects the Philippians with *confidence*. Verse 6: "Being confident of this very thing, that He who has begun a good work in you will complete it until the day of Jesus Christ..." Paul had confidence in God's sustaining and completing grace in the lives of the Philippians. According to his gospel, which the Philippians had embraced with faith, those who are Christ's can be assured that their souls will be carried along throughout this difficult and treacherous life all the way to glory.

In relating to the Philippians his own meditations about them, Paul is reminding them of the *assurance* they can have that God will be faithful to conform them into the image of Jesus Christ. Ultimately, they will be presented before the Father as the spotless bride of His Beloved Son on that Day. You see, Paul is confident that the believers in Philippi will be carried to a Day of perfected sanctification, no matter what ups and downs their lives bring them through. He is confident that the work that has begun in them will be completed because it is *God* who began the work.

Sinclair Ferguson notes regarding this passage that "the good work of the lifelong transformation of these believers has its origin in God. *He began a good work in them*, and, Paul argues, what God begins God completes."[2] When we hear the word "confidence" in the world today, it usually carries the notion of someone who is sure of themselves, someone who is assertive, someone who is full of self-esteem and who has a positive mindset. But this is in no way like the confidence that Paul is describing here. Paul's confidence is rooted in God Himself. It is rooted in what God initiated. It is rooted in God's sovereign decree that has ordained whatsoever comes to pass. It is rooted in God's promises in Christ which have been sealed by the blood of the Son of God. It is rooted in the very words of God Almighty which cannot fail in any way, no matter what dives or dips history takes, no matter what turns in life a believer may encounter.

This is one of the key mindsets we see here in the book of Philippians: the mindset of confidence in God, confidence in Christ, *assurance* that what He has begun He will complete. It is assured confidence that if you are a believer, you will most surely stand on that Day, clothed in the righteousness of our great God and savior, Jesus Christ.

If you are a Christian, have you done something that can dislodge the promise of God in Christ? Have you derailed the holy decree of the Almighty by your sins and shortcomings? Has the fact that you might have harmed your conscience caused your savior, who bought you with His blood, to disown you- you who are inscribed on the palms of His hands? Can anything separate you from the love of Christ? "Shall tribulation, or distress, or persecution, or famine, or nakedness, or peril, or sword?" (Romans 8:35) No, child of God! "I am persuaded that neither death nor life"- life with all of its sins and shortcomings- "nor angels nor principalities nor powers, nor things present nor things to come, nor

---

[2] Sinclair B. Ferguson. *Let's Study Philippians* (Banner of Truth Trust, 2010), 10

height nor depth, nor any other created thing, shall be able to separate us from the love of God which is in Christ Jesus our Lord!" (Romans 8:38-39). Paul recalls the Philippians with this confidence towards God on their behalf.

Have you noted someone struggling in your church? Are you amazed at their weakness, or have you been offended time and time again by their lack of tact, their rudeness at times, or their lack of selflessness? Do you purposely avoid that person? But, I ask you, are they a *Christian*? Do they evidence some grace of God in their life that hints to you that they are indeed a child of God? Remember them in your prayers with *confidence* that you will be standing together with them on that Day.

Perhaps that person may be your spouse or your child who is a believer. When we are offended by one another we must remember who it is that the other person is destined to become if they are a Christian- who it is that they *really* are. That person in your mind is not *really* someone who has offended you- in *reality*, in God's eye, they are the person they are going to be one day: GLORIOUS! Fully reflecting the image of Christ! They will be in full unity and agreement with you in admiring and adoring your Savior and *unable* to offend, *unable* to sin against you for the rest of eternity when that Day comes.

Do you see that person as someone who really deep down inside is also longing for that Day when they will be conformed into the image of Christ? Do you see that your believing spouse, your fellow church member, whoever it is- really deep down inside they want the things you want, they value the things you value, and that they want to *love* you as their brother and as their sister?

You see, you can have confidence that these things are true of every true believer in the Body of Christ. God *will* complete the good work He has already begun. Your brother and your sister are ones Christ died for, ones with whom *God* has originated His plan. They are someone your heavenly Father has ordained to be your companion throughout eternity, someone with whom you will most *assuredly* spend time walking the halls of the palaces of Zion and talking about the glories of the kingdom. For *eternity*! We can have confidence about this! And our confidence should result in love for the brethren. This should be our mindset.

Solidarity

Thirdly, Paul remembers them with *solidarity*. Or rather, he remembers the solidarity they have with him. Verse 7: "just as it is right for me to think this of you all, because I have you in my heart, inasmuch as both in my chains and in the defense and confirmation of the gospel, you all are partakers with me of grace." Remember, Paul is writing from imprisonment in Rome, and he had probably had to face the Roman authorities already to give a defense for himself. The Philippians have shown solidarity with him in all of this. They had sent Epaphroditus (no doubt a cherished member of their own congregation whom they sacrificially sent) who himself risked his own life to find Paul. They had sent a gift to Paul (again, probably monetary) to help him in his hour of need. They had prayed for him. They did not have social media to allow them to track his latest move, but they kept him in their minds and hearts continually, even when they did not have any news regarding his plight. Their hearts were broken for their beloved apostle and they *did* something about it.

Paul held them dear to his own heart because he knew they suffered the same kinds of things he did as a believer in Christ. He could relate to them and they could relate to him in the sufferings for the gospel. And they both did something about it! They prayed for each other, they wrote letters, they travelled grueling distances using ancient modes of travel to get to each other. They loved each other in word *and* deed. They held each other in solidarity.

The *Pocket Oxford American Dictionary &Thesaurus, Third Edition* defines solidarity as: "agreement and support resulting from shared interests, feelings, or opinions." However, we usually hear the term used today in relation to, for example, people in America holding solidarity with a group suffering for democracy in some country under an oppressive regime.

Yet, solidarity should be our mindset with all Christians. Especially with those who are suffering for the gospel. Do you hold solidarity with your brothers and sisters in closed countries? Do you do so in word *and* in deed? Do you *do* something about it? Do we show loving solidarity with suffering Christians around the world? The time may come when Christians we know who live here in America are suffering in chains for the defense and confirmation of the gospel. Are we living a life *now* in such a way that if persecutions happen here, we are ready to risk our necks for the sake of solidarity with our brothers and sisters?

Matthew 25:34-40 reads as follows:

> Then the King will say to those on His right hand, 'Come, you blessed of My Father, inherit the kingdom prepared for you from the foundation of the world: 'for I was hungry and you gave Me food; I was thirsty and you gave Me drink; I was a stranger and you took Me in; I was naked and you clothed Me; I was sick and you visited Me; I was in prison and you came to Me. Then the righteous will answer Him, saying, 'Lord, when did we see You hungry and feed You, or thirsty and give You drink? When did we see You a stranger and take You in, or naked and clothe You? Or when did we see you sick, or in prison, and come to You? And the King will answer and say to them, "Assuredly, I say to you, inasmuch as you did it to one of the least of these My brethren, you did it to Me." Then He will also say to those on the left hand, "Depart from Me, you cursed, into the everlasting fire prepared for the devil and his angels; for I was hungry and you gave Me no food; I was thirsty and you gave Me no drink; I was a stranger and you did not take Me in, naked and you did not clothe Me, sick and in prison and you did not visit Me." Then they also will answer Him, saying, "Lord, when did we see You hungry or thirsty or

a stranger or naked or sick or in prison, and did not minister to You?" Then He will answer them, saying, "Assuredly, I say to you, inasmuch as you did not do it to one of the least of these, you did not do it to Me" And these will go away into everlasting punishment, but the righteous into eternal life.

Are we taking any kind of risks for the sake of solidarity with those who are risking their own necks for the gospel? Do we ever dig down deep in our pockets to send diaconal help to persecuted Christians? Are we daily concerned about missionaries and church planters and their families in our prayer lives? Have we considered refraining from acquiring more stuff at some point and instead using that money to send aid to suffering Christians? Is our unity with other Christians real? Do we consider those in foreign lands living for Christ at great peril as our true brothers and sisters? Do we think of them as part of our family? If we found ourselves suddenly overwhelmed with intense persecution here in America, would we find joy and hold believers in other countries close to our hearts because we knew they held solidarity with us? Would we feel that way if believers in other lands acted the same way we are currently acting towards them?

Perhaps at this point our hearts are bleeding. We might think, "I'm not doing this like I should be." What are we waiting for? More resources? Of course, we must be wise with our money and take care of our families and support our own local church. Neither should we feel that we must make ourselves destitute for the sake of others and bring ourselves into financial ruin. One of the blights of so-called American "Christianity" is the constant abuse of people in fleecing them for their resources and misusing people's hard-earned money for extravagances and luxuries that mar the witness of the church.

The point here is not that we cast our families on skid row for the sake of sending aid to the persecuted. The point is to ask ourselves if our mindset is one that holds solidarity for our brothers and sisters. A mindset that results in love in word *and* deed. We need to preserve unity in our concern for the body of Christ around the world. William Henricksen notes:

> The Philippians had shown that they were deeply concerned in all this. They had prayed for Paul. They had sympathized with him in his experiences- Were not their own experiences similar? Were not they engaged in the same conflict?....And they had even sent their personal representative to him with a gift and in order to assist him in every possible manner.[3]

Affection

Finally, we see Paul remembered the Philippians with *affection*. Verse 8, " For God is my witness, how greatly I long for you all with the affection of Jesus Christ." One of the things that must strike you when you read the epistles of the New Testament is the love which emanates from the writings of the apostles. This was one of the great marks of the early church: Love. Affection. Caring for one another in the name of Jesus Christ. Risking for each other. Sacrificing for each other. When these things are occurring amongst the brethren, it is hard for there not to be great tenderness towards each other.

Jesus said in John 13:35, "By this all will know that you are My disciples, if you have love for one another." Jesus is not just saying here, "love one another in sacrificing for each other and doing good deeds" (all things that we need to be doing). The love of the brethren is not in coldly writing a check for tithes and offerings with little or no feeling, or in donating items out of a sense of mere duty; but these things are all done in love that also displays itself in *affection*.

Churches can get so stuffy, so snobby, so pious at times. A visitor walks in and they might enjoy the reverence given to God in the service, but perhaps they end up leaving because they do not sense any affection

---

[3] William Hendriksen. *Galatians, Ephesians, Philippians, Colossians, and Philemon, New Testament Commentary* (Baker Academic, 1962), 57

from the brethren there. Sometimes you have to be a part of the "inner circle" before you can know tenderness from the brethren. Sometimes in churches, grudges are held when offenses come. Affection becomes cold.

> Therefore, as the elect of God, holy and beloved, put on tender mercies, kindness, humility, meekness, longsuffering; bearing with one another, and forgiving one another, if anyone has a complaint against another; even as Christ forgave you, so you also must do.(Coloss. 3:12, 13)

There needs to be affection amongst us as Christians. Affection also for those we know in other churches. Paul greatly *longed* for the Philippians. Do you feel that way about any other believers? The Greek word here for affection is *splagchnois*, and it has a very forceful sense of deep love for someone personally with one's whole being. The *Theological Dictionary of the New Testament* notes: "the word is again used for the whole person which in the depths of its emotional life has experienced refreshment through consolation and love."[4] The word really means love, but it is different from *agape* in that it expresses "the mutual experience and gift among Christians."[5]

Have we become members of the church with this mindset? Or do we come to our churches on a Lord's Day and see other people there as mere acquaintances whom we could do with or without? If you are a Christian, you must have known the affection of Jesus Christ for other believers at some point. This is one of the church's greatest witnesses to the world. That is how the world will know that God is amongst us: by our love for one another. "By this all will know that you are my disciples if you have love for one another"(John 13:35) "That they may be one, as You, Father, are in Me, and I in You; that they also may be one in Us, that the world may believe that You sent Me"(John 17:21)

---

[4] Gerhard Kittel, Gerhard Friedrich eds. *Theological Dictionary of the New Testament vol. VII* (Wm. B. Eerdmans Publishing Company, 1999), 555
[5] Ibid., 556

This is how Christianity spreads. This is how it spread in the early church even in the midst of persecutions: through the supernatural affection between those who were united in the fellowship of the gospel. This should be our mindset. *Joy* in our fellowship together for the sake of the gospel, *confidence* in God's promise to carry us to glory, *solidarity* with one another- especially in our sufferings for Christ; and underneath it all with the great *affections* of Jesus Christ for one another.

This is our first taste of the Philippians mindset. The next nine chapters will continue to help us through the pinnacles and pitfalls we encounter as we strive to live the Christian life. Meditating on this mindset will give us the ability to discern between good and evil in the midst of this crooked generation in which we find ourselves trying to be a witness. May God help us as we study further.

Chapter Two

And this I pray, that your love may abound still more and more in knowledge and in all discernment, that you may approve the things that are excellent, that you may be sincere and without offense till the day of Christ, being filled with the fruits of righteousness which are by Jesus Christ, to the glory and praise of God- Phil. 1:9-11

The world today is concerned about the *heart*. They encourage one another to be true to their heart. The songs and philosophies of the world emphasize that we be led by the feelings of our heart. Love is held high in the world's esteem. Everything should be done in the name of love, we often hear, and love comes from the heart, so they say.

Elated emotions and warm feelings are the engines of the entertainment industry. Good feelings are what can addict people to drugs, they can be how people "hook up" at bars, and they are what draw people back over and over again to the party life. People desire to have their hearts full of happiness and joy, and they so often seek fulfillment in what the world has to offer in warming up their feelings.

Emotion, the heart, and love are all things that are commended in the Bible. Love the Lord your God with all your heart and love your neighbor as yourself are the two greatest commandments. As we saw in the last chapter, Paul greatly longed for the church in Philippi with the affection of Jesus Christ. So, loving, knowing warmth of elation of emotion, having a full heart- these are not bad things in themselves. These are aspects to God creating us in His image. This is part of the nobility of humanity.

In fact, Paul here wants the Philippians' love to abound more and more for each other and for God. But biblical love is something that is engaged in, something that is stirred up by, something that is guided by the *mind*. Paul wants their love to abound more and more in *knowledge* and all *discernment*. Paul desires the Philippians to grow in their knowledge of how to love and to be discerning in the way they love.

All of humanity has been ruined by sin. Our minds have been ravaged by deception, perversion, and wickedness. The world claims it values love and claims it is guided by the heart; but love, emotions, and heart must take their cues from the mind. They only follow the mindset that has been determined by the human will. Love flows out of the values, the priorities, that a man or woman, boy or girl has determined within their minds and by their wills- whether they are conscious of having done so or not. The world's love, and the heart of humanity is therefore severely mis-guided. It is warped and twisted. The Scripture says that the heart is deceitfully wicked above all things, because the minds of the peoples of this world are in slavery and in bondage to sin.

There might be very philanthropic gestures made by upstanding citizens in the world and there might be couples who love each other and have stayed married for decades. But, ultimately, if the mind has not been renewed by the regenerating power of the Holy Spirit and if individuals have not realized they are sinners and have turned to Christ alone for salvation from the wrath it deserves, then all their acts of love and goodness will be at their deepest roots actually only selfish, or lustful, and set against the glory of God.

For the Christian, Paul says in Romans: "... do not be conformed to this world, but be transformed by the renewing of your mind, that you may prove what is that good and acceptable and perfect will of God" (Rom. 12:2). All of the Christian life is learning to exercise our senses to discern what is good and what is evil. It is being able to understand more and more the will of God. We are learning how to love! Paul says we must do this through knowledge and discernment.

We get the knowledge of how to love and we become more discerning in our love by saturating ourselves in the Word of God. But we cannot simply go out and buy a Bible and start a reading schedule. We cannot simply listen to sermons about the word of God, either. We should not just show up to the church service on a Lord's Day. We cannot sleepily read a chapter of the Bible before we turn out the light at night. What does Paul say here in this verse? "AND THIS I PRAY" (capitalization mine).

How badly do you want to grow in knowledge and discernment of the will of God? Are you *praying* that God would grant you this? Are you praying throughout the week that God would speak to you on the coming Lord's Day? How badly do you want this? Paul wanted it so bad that he desired for those he loved to have it too. He knew it was paramount to the Christian life that love would abound! Paul understood it was essential that the will of God would be discerned by the church of Jesus Christ. Christians need to cry out to God in prayer daily that He would give them knowledge and discernment. Get on your knees and ask Him to transform your mind. Do it daily! Open your Bible in the evenings or in the mornings with a confession to God in prayer that you desperately need Him to enlighten your understanding as to how to love more and more.

Proverbs 2:3-6 says this:

> If you call out for insight and raise your voice for understanding, if you seek it like silver and search for it as for hidden treasures, then you will understand the fear of the LORD and find the knowledge of God. For the LORD gives wisdom; from His mouth come knowledge and understanding.

How badly do you want to grow in love? Do you feel stunted in your Christian growth? Do you feel as though you are dull and unfeeling towards the ways of God? Perhaps, my friend, your plateauing in the Christian life is due to you not wanting it bad enough. Oh, we mourn and cry out when we make a fool of ourselves. But how often do we cry out to God in prayerful desperation for insight, understanding, and for the treasures of wisdom and knowledge in Christ? Are we too polite and proper for this? Are we too composed to express ourselves this way in our homes? Do we blush at the idea of weeping before the Lord in prayer even when we are alone?

Again, I say, our lack of growth in the Christian life has to do with *us*. It has to do with our attitudes towards the word of God. It has to do with our lack of knowledge and discernment. We lack this because we do not stir up ourselves and motivate ourselves to seek God in prayer for these things. Not just once, not just twice. But as Paul says: "Pray without ceasing".

The following is from a helpful passage in a little booklet by Roger Ellsworth called *Come Down, LORD!*:

> The problem, according to the Bible, is not at God's end. This same prophet tells us: '…the Lord longs to be gracious to you, and therefore he waits on high to have compassion on you' (Isa. 30:18). The Psalmist pictures it like this: 'How great is thy goodness, which Thou hast stored up for those who fear thee, …'(Psa. 31:19). Verses like these prompted the great Charles Spurgeon to exclaim: "God is ready to help. He has everything in preparation before our need begin. He has laid in supplies for all our wants. Before our prayers are presented, he has prepared answers to them;…' "If the problem is not with God, then who is left? We are! If we are not enjoying God's power, it is because we are not utilizing the channel God has provided for receiving his power. What is that channel? It is right here in Isaiah's prayer. The prophet says God ' acts in behalf of the one who waits for him' Waiting on God, then, is the bridge between God's power and our need.[6]

---

[6] Roger Ellsworth. *Come Down, Lord!* (Banner of Truth Trust, 2009), 18

Now, waiting on God does not mean we just wait and do nothing. Think more of the idea of a good waiter in a restaurant. In this restaurant, the waiter communicates with God (the customer) through prayer, and God communicates with the waiter through His Word. Therefore, to wait upon God is to seek Him in prayer and hang upon His every word! The Philippians mindset here is to seek God for knowledge and discernment in how to live, love, and how to serve Jesus Christ.

Is daily life a series of labors and joys, loving family and friends, enjoying hobbies- aspects of daily living that for you are leading up to a time of prayer and meditation in God's word as the *pinnacle* of your day? Or are other things, other people- are these things you love and value more than spending time with the Lord Jesus Christ? Is time drawing near to God a necessary burden or hassle for you? There is something seriously wrong if that is the case.

Jesus said in Luke 14:26, "If anyone comes to me and does not hate his father and mother, wife and children, brothers and sisters, yes, and his own life also, he cannot be My disciple." We know Jesus is not saying don't love your children, your wife, or your life. But in a provocative way he is saying that your desire and love for God and His ways should far exceed your love for anything else. We can actually love God through loving our families, working to His glory, and having creative hobbies that glorify Him for giving us gifts. But if indeed we are doing all these things to the glory of God, as we should, then something is wrong if prayer and meditation in the Word of God is a burden. Something is backwards.

Let us instead grow in our knowledge and discernment of love, as Paul lays out this mindset. When our minds are renewed in how to love God's way, we will be able to do three things: We will be able to identify goodness; we will be able to be genuine; and we will be able to bear fruit.

Identifying Goodness

First of all, when our love abounds in knowledge and discernment, we will be able to identify goodness: "and this I pray, that your love may abound more and more in knowledge and all discernment *that you may approve the things that are excellent"* (Phil. 1:9, 10a). Our minds in the Christian life, throughout our process of sanctification, and as we are being conformed into the image of Jesus Christ, should be continually sharpened to discern the things that are excellent as opposed to those things that are evil.

Sound simple? To know what is right and what is wrong? If it were so simple, then why do we go on sinning every day? We need to grow in our *approval* of the things that are excellent, you see. We need to grow in our fondness and favor towards the good things of Christ. We need to learn the will of God, the way of His love, and discern its worthiness. We need to approve the things that are excellent!

Hebrews 6:14 says, "But solid food belongs to those who are of full age, that is, those who by reason of practice have their senses exercised to discern both good and evil." Romans 12:2 says, "And do not be conformed to this world, but be transformed by the renewing of your minds, that you may prove what is that *good* and *acceptable* and *perfect will* of God" (italics mine). Our senses need to be exercised through the transforming power of the Word of God showing us and revealing to us the worthiness of God's ways. Our problem in the Christian life is not so much knowing what is right and what is wrong, but it is actually approving of the will of God within our heart of hearts.

Do we see God's ways as good and acceptable? Do we recognize their perfections? Do we feel we lack in our ability to love? Does our pride so often come to the surface in our daily relationships and actions that we fumble our witness, stain our good works, and people smell smoke when we attempt to die to ourselves? Well, the problem is that we don't approve what is excellent enough in our hearts. Our senses are not exercised to discern the wickedness in our attitudes enough so that we resist sin. Our senses are not acute enough to cause us to fight for faith or to run from temptation.

So often the case is that we justify ourselves. We excuse ourselves. We deceive ourselves into believing things we know deep down inside are contrary to God's ways. We tell ourselves these twisted ways and attitudes are OK, that God understands, and that they will not cause any harm. We believe that they are a neutral action.

Of course, God is patient, and He is kind. He knows we are unable to untwist ourselves completely from sin during this life. But let us examine ourselves. Are there some attitudes, some tendencies of speaking, some ways we meditate, some things we engage in that as we read, we are coming to realize there are aspects to our character which need pruning? As David prayed in so many words, "Search my heart and show me if there is any wicked way I'm entertaining in my life".

Do we want to grow in the grace and knowledge of the Lord Jesus Christ? Have we plateaued for some time now? Grow in your discernment, dear Christian. Approve what is excellent and compare it with your own ways. Is it time to shed those certain aspects of your character today? Have you had a serious time of repentance before God lately? We must know that we have to experience continual change as Christians. We cannot get too comfortable with our habits of character. God calls us to repent, to turn to Him over and over again- afresh and anew. He calls us to shed coats of sinful tendencies we previously were not aware of.

We are to grow in maturity, we are to eat solid food, and we are to grow in discerning and in the knowledge of the will of God. We are to conform our lives to that will. We can reach plateaus from time to time in the Christian life, but if we are not seeking to grow in knowledge and discernment and we are not seeking how to abound more and more in love and obedience to God's will, then we are in danger of our profession of faith in Christ being one of hypocrisy.

Listen to Thomas Watson in *the Godly Man's Picture*:

> This is one great difference between a child of God and a hypocrite. The hypocrite picks and chooses in religion. He will perform some duties which are easier and gratify his pride or interest, but other duties he takes no notice of: 'Ye pay tithe

and mint and anise, and have omitted the weightier matters of the law, judgement, mercy, and faith' (matt 23:23). To sweat in some duties of religion and freeze in others is the symptom of a disordered Christian. Jehu was zealous in destroying the idolatry of Baal, but let the golden calves of Jeroboam stand. This shows that men are not good in truth when they are good by halves.[7]

Can you approve the things that are excellent? Are you at least growing in this? Do you identify goodness?

Being Genuine

The second thing we will be able to do if we are growing in our knowledge and discernment of love is that we will be able to be genuine. Paul says, "that you may approve the things that are excellent, *that you may be sincere and without offense till the day of Christ*" (Phil. 1:10, italics mine). The word for sincere is *eilichrineis*, which means "pure". The sentence could be translated: In order that you may be pure and blameless in preparation for the day of Christ.[8] The idea, as Peter T. O'Brien points out in his commentary, is that the Philippians be prepared for judgment day in a positive and in a negative sense. Pure, in the positive sense. And blameless, in the negative sense. The Philippians, in other words, need to live genuine Christian lives- they cannot be false professors and think they will stand on the day of judgment.

Now, we know that sinners are justified before God because they have faith in Christ alone, not by works of righteousness. They are clothed in the righteousness of Christ which is freely given to them by the grace of God through faith in His name. Nothing we do can earn us right standing on judgment day. But we also know that James says that if our faith is not accompanied by works, then our faith is dead. We cannot

---

[7] Thomas Watson. *The Godly Man's Picture* (Banner of Truth Trust, 2013), 167
[8] Peter T. O'Brien. *The Epistle to the Philippians, the New International Greek Testament Commentary* (Wm. B. Eerdmans Publishing Co., 1991), 78

merely confess with our mouth that Jesus is Lord and not follow Him by repenting of our sins and seeking to do His will. We cannot say we are Christians and not long for God's will to be accomplished in our lives. We are not genuine believers if we do not desire to grow in knowledge and discernment in ways to love and glorify God and in ways to love our neighbors.

Paul says, if we long to grow in this knowledge, we will be able to manifest genuine Christian lives. We will seek to be pure- to be *sincere*, it can be translated. Our lives are to reflect the holiness of God. O'Brien notes that the term for "sincere" in secular Greek signified the absence of alloy. No impurities in the gold, in other words. Now immediately, our minds should recall the many passages of Scripture that talk about God refining His people. Often, the purity of our faith is tested, in other words. Our faith is tested, usually, through the trials we endure in this life. Remember Peter's words in 1 Peter 1:6-7:

> In this you greatly rejoice, though now for a little while, if need be, you have been grieved by various trials, that the genuineness of your faith, being much more precious than gold that perishes, though it is tested by fire, may be found to praise, honor, and glory at the revelation of Jesus Christ.

The mindset we are to have as Christians is one of seeking to trust God in all circumstances. Our faith must remain pure throughout life's difficulties. We cannot jettison faith in Christ when times get rough. We cannot put our trust for salvation in anything that tempts to lure us away from sufficiency in Christ alone. We must stay genuine for the entire race. Our faith must be precious to us, as it is precious to God. We must protect it and strive to keep it pure.

Furthermore, in a negative sense, we must be blameless. We must keep ourselves unspotted from the world. We must conduct ourselves in such a way that we are without offence against the ways of Christ and free from serious and scandalous sins. The mindset of the Christian must be to be watchful and serious in guarding ourselves. We are to discern the heads of pathways that lead to destruction. We are to be knowledgeable about the ways of the world, not in a way that we are rehearsed in its evils, but in a way that is able to see where its principles will lead. We cannot be ignorant of the devil's devices. We cannot be fools and think we will be without any offence if we adopt the world's ways or if we allow ourselves to be seduced by the things that this world values.

Now, thank God, we take on this mindset, and we seek to be pure and blameless as Christians, with the knowledge that if we are His we *will* persevere to the end. This is the gospel of Jesus Christ: that He will complete the good work He started in us. We fight from victory. In our striving to be like Christ we are backed by the promise that we most certainly will be like Him one day.

Wilhemus A Brakel writes:

> It is this doctrine which underscores all comforts which believers derive from other doctrines of the faith. For what comfort can be found in the fact that one is regenerated, has been adopted as a child of God, and has received the forgiveness of sin, if he knows that tomorrow he may be a child of the devil and of hell again? If, however, along with the reception of grace, one is assured that he shall be kept by the power of God, that the covenant is immutable, and that he shall most certainly become a partaker of eternal felicity- only then will grace truly yield him joy, will he be quickened in love, and can he forget what is behind him and reach forth to that which is before him, pressing 'toward the mark for the prize of the high calling of God.'[9]

So, we are called to develop the mindset Paul lays out here in the book of Philippians. This is the mindset he prays the Philippians would cultivate. But we thank God, that there is One who sits at the right hand of God,

---

[9] Wilhelmus A Brakel. *The Christian's Reasonable Service, vol. 4* (Reformation Heritage Books, 1995), 296

who has already lived out this mindset perfectly. There is One who has purchased with His own blood His church which He has promised to make into His likeness on that Day. We follow Paul as he followed Christ, who has blazed the trail of the perfect mindset already before us. We must keep in mind, with all of the imperatives we have been considering, that it is Christ alone who lived a life of perfect, sinless, godly mindsets.

And yet, if we are His, we will seek to abound more and more in a way to love through knowledge and discernment. When we do so, we will be able to identify goodness more and more. With this mindset we will be able to live genuine Christian lives until the race is finished, and we will be able to be fruitful as well. Paul says, again,

> And this I pray, that your love may abound still more and more in knowledge and discernment, that you may approve the things that are excellent, that you may be sincere and without offense till the day of Christ, BEING FILLED WITH THE FRUITS OF RIGHTEOUSNESS which are by Jesus Christ, to the glory and praise of God (Phil. 1:9-11, capitalization mine)

A genuine Christian will bear fruit, the fruits of righteousness. This is the evidence that they have been justified in Christ Jesus. Fruits are the marks and signs that they have truly been clothed in the righteousness of Christ. The Bible says that without holiness, no one will see the Lord (Heb. 12:14). You cannot enter heaven unless you have some resemblance of godliness, holiness, and fruitfulness to the glory of God.

As Christians we need to desire this. We need to *seek* to bear fruit. We realize this is elementary Christianity. But can those of us who feel these are truths too basic for our own consideration recognize in our daily events at the end of each day that God indeed bore fruit through us? This is not something prideful. This is essential to genuine Christianity. If we think we are being humble by declaring we never bear fruit to God's glory, we are mistaken. The genuine Christian *must* bear fruit. We must live and produce evidence that our faith is not a dead faith.

You probably remember well the words of Jesus in John 15:

> I am the true vine, and My Father is the vinedresser. Every branch in Me that does not bear fruit He takes away; and every branch that bears fruit He prunes, that it may bear more fruit … Abide in Me, and I in you. As the branch cannot bear fruit of itself, unless it abides in the vine, neither can you, unless you abide in Me. I am the vine, you are the branches. He who abides in Me, and I in him, bears much fruit; for without Me you can do nothing (Jn. 15:1-2; 4-5).

Now, of course, brothers and sisters, we are *weak*. We do not glorify God nearly as we should. We are pale, ghostly comparisons to the Man Christ Jesus. Yet we must bear some resemblance to Him if we are truly His. We must bear the fruits of righteousness. We must desire this. And if we are appalled at our lack of fruitfulness at this point in our lives, my friends, then it is doubtful we have sought to abide in Jesus as we should. Why is it we try to do, and to accomplish, and to provide for and to labor and to minister- yet in the process we set aside and compromise fellowship with Christ? We grow slack in the meditation and study of His Word, and in seeking and waiting upon Him in prayer. At this point we should realize all the more that we can do nothing without Christ.

As believers, it is essential that we cultivate a mindset which results in being fruitful to the glory of God. And we cannot bear fruit unless we are abiding in Christ, keeping close accounts with Him and drawing near to Him through the means of grace.

Listen to Thomas Brooks in the classic work called *Precious Remedies against Satan's Devices*. He writes,

> If you would not be taken with any of Satan's snares and devices, then keep up your communion with God. Your strength

to stand and withstand Satan's fiery darts is from your communion with God. A soul high in communion with God may be tempted, but will not easily be conquered. Such a soul will fight it out to the death....Communion with Christ is very inflaming, raising and strengthening. While Samson kept up his communion with God, no enemy could stand before him, but he goes on conquering and to conquer; but when he was fallen in his communion with God, he quickly falls before the plots of his enemies. It will be so with your souls. So long as your communion with God is kept up, you will be too hard for 'spiritual wickedness in high places'; but if you fall from your communion with God, you will fall, as others, before the face of every temptation.[10]

I would add this: Christians who are deep in communion with God not only are greatly insulated from Satan's attacks and temptations, but they are able to abound in the fruits of righteousness to the glory of God. Those who abide in the true vine, will bear fruit. Is this our daily concern? Are you looking daily, praying daily, for God to bear fruit through you to His glory? It needs to be so if we would name the name of Christ.

Paul prayed that these things would be evident in the lives of the church members of Philippi. He asked God that this would be their mindset. His concern was that they abound still more and more in their love- love for Christ, love for the church, and love for the world. Their mindset was to be one of knowledge and discernment in the ways of Christ.

We cannot remain satisfied in the ruts we settle into. It would be to our relief and benefit if we sought to trim off the excesses of the flesh in our souls. Repenting afresh and anew and drawing near to the Lord Jesus Christ is our calling. He is the paradigm of One who approves what is excellent and who lived a life of true genuine godliness and bore fruits of righteousness.

---

[10] Thomas Brooks. *Precious Remedies Against Satan's Devices* (Banner of Truth Trust, 2011), 248

As we study this Philippians mindset, we should feel overwhelmed. We cannot do this! We cannot live the Christian life! We fail so deeply in imitating Paul and fulfilling the mindset he prayed for the church to have! But, this is a good place to be, this is a good thing to realize, dear Christian. Without Christ, you can do nothing. Go to Him for strength in your weakness. Go to Him for forgiveness of sins and failures. Go to Him to be clothed in His righteousness. Christ *alone*! Yes, we must have some kind of resemblance of these mindsets if we are to truly be called Christians. But it is Jesus, *only* Jesus who holds out the way of God for us. He is the way, the truth, and the life. In Him are all the treasures of wisdom and knowledge.

Paul said in Ephesians 2:10 that we are "*His* workmanship, created in Christ Jesus for good works, which God prepared beforehand that we should walk in them." We can only walk in the footsteps of Christ by placing our feet within the prints He has left on the trail. We cannot produce any righteousness of our own. The fruits of righteousness are the good works which God prepared in Christ for us to be able to participate in. To God be the glory!

We live in the midst of a crooked and perverse generation. Only Christ, only the word of God can bring any kind of hope to this lost world. Let us greatly desire to abound in love, in knowledge and all discernment; to shed our own sinful likeness, more and more, so that we are replaced with the image of Jesus Christ. We hold this treasure in earthen vessels. As the church of Christ, we are a frail, sinful humanity, holding within our souls the light of the world, the Son of God who *alone* can bring redemption to lost sinners.

Chapter Three

For I know that this will turn out for my deliverance through your prayer and the supply of the Spirit of Jesus Christ, according to my earnest expectation and hope that in nothing I shall be ashamed, but with all boldness, as always, so now also Christ will be magnified in my body, whether by life or by death. For to me, to live is Christ, and to die is gain. But if I live on in the flesh, this will mean fruit from my labor, yet what I shall choose I cannot tell. For I am hard-pressed between the two, having a desire to depart and be with Christ, which is far better. Nevertheless to remain in the flesh is more needful for you. And being confident of this, I know that I shall remain and continue with you all for your progress and joy of faith, that your rejoicing for me may be more abundant in Jesus Christ by my coming to you again. Philippians 1:19-26

In the mini-series about some of the latter days of WW2, called *Band of Brothers*, there is an episode where many of the men who are fighting are amazed at one particular soldier's incredible bravery and success in battle. These men cannot understand how this particular soldier has such nerve during combat, or how he can resolve to do the things he does in the midst of frightening situations. At one point, this extraordinary soldier tells them his secret. "I'm already dead," he says. You see, because he figured he was already dead, already going to be killed in battle, all of his hesitation and fears and anxieties had been washed away.

The Christian life would have us don a similar way of thinking. Whether we live or we die, we do all to the glory of God. To live is Christ, to die is gain. We have been crucified to the world, and now we have nothing to lose. Going hard after God will not see us lose out on anything of eternal worth but will see us gain riches in Christ's kingdom forever.

The crux of this passage is in verses 20 and 21, where Paul declares that he is filled with expectation that in nothing he shall be ashamed because he knows Christ will be magnified whether he lives or he dies. For him, to live is Christ, to die is gain.

This book is looking at the mindset Paul lays out throughout the book of Philippians. What we are calling the Philippians mindset. The Christian life is won or lost in the battle over our minds. Indeed, Scripture has a lot to say about how we should conduct our thought-lives. Though there are other doctrines to be found in the book of Philippians, in this book we are attempting to draw out from the text what mental words Paul is weaving into these themes. Again, to grow in the grace and knowledge of the Lord Jesus Christ means that our senses are to be exercised in such a way that, more and more, we will be able to discern good and evil. We will be able to prove what is that good and perfect will of God through the transforming of our minds.

We saw back in chapter one that Paul remembered the Philippians in prayer with joy. He filled his mind with a confidence about the fact that God would complete the work He had started in the Philippians. His mind was filled with remembrance in joy for the fact that the Philippians were participating in the cause of the kingdom along with Paul. We saw that Paul remembered the Philippians with joy, secondly with confidence, third that he did it with solidarity, and finally that he did it with affection.

In chapter two we studied how Paul was desiring for the Philippians' love to grow in *knowledge* and *discernment*, our next set of mental words. To grow in knowledge and discernment in the way we love, we must first approve the things that are excellent, secondly that we may be sincere and without offence till the day of Christ, and finally that we may be filled with the fruits of righteousness.

Now we are pressing on deeper into the 1st chapter of Philippians, and once again, we find a pair of mental words in our text. Actually, it is the same word repeated in verse 19 and in verse 25: it is the word "know". Verse 19 says, "For I *know* that this will turn out for my deliverance through your prayer and the supply of the Spirit of Jesus Christ." Verse 25 says, "And being confident of this, I *know* that I shall remain and continue with you all for your progress and joy of faith." These two occasions of our mental word "know" are the bookends, or we might say that they contain the bread of the sandwich. In the middle of the sandwich we read of the meat of verses 20 and 21- the crux of the passage, which culminates in the declaration Paul is so famous for "For to me, to live is Christ, and to die is gain."

Assurance of Deliverance

The first thing we notice in this sandwich is that in verse 19 Paul was *assured of deliverance*. Here is the historical context of this passage: Paul is under house arrest in Rome. He has appealed to Ceasar while a prisoner in Ceasarea, in Palestine. After his perilous journey to Rome where he was shipwrecked, the Romans allowed him to rent a house while he awaited his trial, albeit as a prisoner under the guard of Roman soldiers. But Paul was allowed to have visitors, and to write letters, and to receive guests such as Epaphroditus from Philippi who brought him a gift to help him in his hour of need.

No doubt, Paul was dripping with evangelistic zeal during his imprisonment, so much so that we read in 1:12-14,

> But I want you to know, brethren, that the things which happened to me have actually turned out for the furtherance of the gospel, so that it has become evident to the whole palace guard, and to all the rest, that my chains are in Christ: and most of the brethren in the Lord, having become confident by my chains, are much more bold to speak the word without fear.

So here we have Paul experiencing a major inconvenience: He is a prisoner. He is chained to soldiers. He is praying that God will provide for him. He needs money to rent the house, for food and clothing. He cannot go out and work as a tentmaker to provide for himself at this point. He has been burdened with bringing the gospel to the Gentiles, but there is this major inconvenience he is experiencing: Financial hardship. Temptations for anxiety. Longing to see loved ones.

But Paul, instead of allowing his circumstances to trample upon his countenance, just exudes with all his heart the message and joy of the gospel. He takes the bull by the horns, so much so that the palace guard, Ceasar's own soldiers, have heard and understood the gospel. Why is Paul in chains? For the sake of Jesus Christ who died for sinners. Paul is living and breathing this message of hope. Paul is producing fruit wherever he goes! The brethren who hear of his predicament are emboldened by Paul's fearlessness and confidence in the midst of suffering, and so they go out preaching the gospel as well.

Paul is also filled with the assurance of deliverance. He *knows* that through the prayers of the church and the supply of the Spirit he will be delivered. The Greek word for "deliverance" in verse 19 is the word for "salvation". The question is, what does Paul believe he will be *saved* from here? We might naturally think according to the context just mentioned, that Paul means he will be delivered from imprisonment, that he will be saved from this trial he is about to experience before Ceasar. This seems to flow in line with the context very well.

However, Sinclair Ferguson points out that Paul is more than likely referencing his Greek Old Testament, where this same Greek word is used in Job 13:16. Job 13:13-16 reads as follows:

> Hold your peace with me, and let me speak, then let come on me what may! Why do I take my flesh in my teeth, and put my life in his hands? Though He slay me, yet will I trust Him. Even so, I will defend my own ways before Him. He also shall be my SALVATION, for a hypocrite could not come before Him (Capitalization mine).

There in Job 13, Job is confident that God will be His deliverance, his salvation at the judgment seat. And though Paul feels assurance he will be delivered from the judgment seat of Ceasar, he is filled with an even greater *assurance* that he will be delivered from the judgment seat of God Almighty- that the supply of the Spirit of Christ will carry Him through to the end of his fight of faith. Paul knows that whatever happens there in Rome, ultimately, he will be delivered, he will be saved.

To Live is Christ, To Die is Gain

The question is then asked: According to what? How does Paul know this? We read in verse 20: "according to my earnest expectation and hope that in nothing I shall be ashamed, but with all boldness as always, so now also Christ will be magnified in my body, whether by life or death."

Paul knows he will be delivered because he is filled with the mindset that he is already dead. It doesn't matter if he lives or if he dies- Christ will be magnified either way. We see this is Paul's earnest expectation and hope, that in nothing he will be ashamed. Paul quotes Isaiah in Romans 9:33: "As it is written: 'Behold I lay in Zion a stumbling stone and rock of offense, and whoever believes on Him will not be put to shame". And then again, in Romans 10:11 He says, "For the Scripture says, 'Whoever believes on Him will not be put to shame".

You see, Paul's earnest expectation and hope that he would not be ashamed was his faith in the gospel of Jesus Christ. This is his assurance of deliverance. For the sinner who has been given the light of the knowledge of Jesus Christ, for former blasphemers to suddenly know that they have been rescued permanently from the wrath of God, for those who lived under the fear of death because they were slaves of sin to be given faith in the forgiveness that is in Christ Jesus- this means that you are filled with hope and expectation in life. It means that despair has been whisked away as the curtains that have darkened your room of existence are suddenly pulled aside and you see the light of the glory of God in the face of Jesus Christ. Suddenly, the sinner is given a new heart that loves God with all the soul, all the mind- and that sinner is filled with a realization that they will never face shame at the judgment seat of God on that Day.

It is not that the Christian who knows this never faces any fears again, or never faces any temptations to despair, or will no longer have doubts. But the gospel of Jesus Christ again and again brings in this light of assurance of deliverance to the sinner- over and over again. So much so, that when you are determining to exude the gospel, to drip with evangelistic zeal because the joy of the Lord is your strength, you will become so saturated with gospel truth that you will keep short accounts with Christ. The truth of what he did on the cross for sinners will reverberate constantly in your soul. As you tell others of the joy you've found, as you remember others in prayer, as you grow in knowledge and discernment in your love, you will find that in the midst of inconvenience, in the midst of trials, in the midst of suffering, the assurance that in nothing you will be ashamed will flood your soul.

Did Paul really know what the outcome of his trial would be before Ceasar at this point? I do not think that he did. But Paul did not really care, because he was clinging to the gospel of Jesus Christ. To live for Christ is the most freeing life because you have died to the world and its principles, your citizenship is in heaven, and you are under the mindset that your life is at God's disposal. Should Christ keep you to remain laboring in the fight of faith, you know that you will bear fruit to His glory. Should your life be cut off, you face assurance that you will stand before your redeemer unashamed, welcomed into eternal joys of the never-ending Sabbath Day.

"For to me to live is Christ, and to die is gain". Paul had been set free from all of the entanglements of idols. No longer did he live for his own glory or for any other idol. Now to live was Christ! A singular focus.

What are we living for? Perhaps we began to work to provide for our families in the name of Christ, to work to provide for God's kingdom, to experience recreation to enjoy God in the good things he has given us and to keep us healthy for the glory of God. Perhaps we began the

Christian life with the aim to live for Christ, and all the responsibilities we tacked on to our lives were originally for that aim. Maybe that aim was regarding ministries we are involved in. We started teaching Sunday School, we started playing a musical instrument, we started serving in the kitchen, we became a deacon or a pastor- all with the aim of living for Christ.

But what happens to us so often? The means to glorify God becomes an end in itself. We get so caught up in the vehicles to enjoy God, that we entangle ourselves with self-seeking, with idolatries, with joy-less serving, with duty- drudgery. In the name of raising our children in the ways of Christ we miss out on developing a relationship with them where we can walk with God together in love and harmony. We hammer out a way to provide for our spouses, and we miss loving them as Christ loved the church. We come to church to be faithful attenders, but the joy of the Lord, the expectation of drawing near to Him in worship has been lost.

How did Paul carry the badge: to live is Christ? He kept himself close to the gospel. He kept short accounts with Christ, the One who came and bled for his sins. He meditated on the assurance he had of salvation, of deliverance from the wrath to come. He had an earnest expectation and hope that he would stand on that Day of judgment. He slew all his fears in life with the determination that "Though he slay me, yet I will trust Him" (Job 13:15). Paul lives the Christian life as though he were already dead. Dead to anything that would deviate him from living for Christ. Dead to all the idols that tried to tempt him to serving them. Dead to desire for fame and fortune. Dead to desire for his own exaltation. And with a knowledge that should he die physically, it would only be gain. To die, is gain. A man with this kind of mindset is absolutely unstoppable.

But would it truly be gain for Paul to die? Think of all that depended on him in the early church. How could the churches go on without him? Think about what you would do if your spouse were to die. How could you go on without them? What would happen to your children if they suddenly had no mother? What would happen if the bread winner of the family were suddenly cut off? How can that be *gain*? Paul must only mean here in this verse, *his* gain. Of course, he is going to gain! He will be in glory, he will be at rest, he will be sinless, he will be with Christ! But it will not be gain for those he has left behind, will it?

There will surely be loss and mourning and sorrow when a saint dies in the Lord. There will be hardships for those who are left behind. But we know, that "whate'er my God ordains is right"[11]. That means that no matter who dies, if you are Christ's and you are left behind, God has a purpose that you will thank Him for when you get to glory. When you meet your loved one again on the other side of the Jordan and join with them never to be parted again, you will realize that you have been molded and shaped into the glorious image of Jesus Christ through your hardships and sorrows in a way that nothing else could have. Christ has become precious to you in a way He could not have if your Paul had remained. Your character has had its impurities refined so that you are able to shine as gold on that Day. All your sorrows, all your mourning, all your difficulties will be forgotten as the pure and holy joy of reunited love in Christ washes over you for all eternity.

You see, death is gain for the Christian who is left behind because it is only temporary. The waiting we experience in suffering and longing will make glory unspeakably glorious. "For our light affliction, which is but for a moment, is working for us a far more exceeding and eternal weight of glory" (2 Cor. 4:17). As Christians, we are to live like we are dead, and die like we are going to live forever. To live is Christ! To die is only gain. No doubt gain for the one being ushered into the presence of Christ in sinless perfection and holiness, but also, gain for those left behind. It is only temporary, all the while working a weight of glory as we wait to be reunited with those we love in the Lord.

One of the things that has always put a lump in my throat is that each of my sons when they were little would get so sad when they would wake

---

[11] From the old hymn by Samuel Rodigast, 1675.

up on a weekday morning and realize I had gone to work. I remember the boys looking out the window as I drove off to my job and waving to them knowing they were crying. But it is only temporary. I get to come home each day and see them. Saturday mornings, when my son wakes up and realizes Dad is home- well, it's a sweet reunion of sorts for us. How much more to see those who have passed on before us again, never to be separated for all eternity.

To die in the Lord is gain, my friends. We should relish in that! To be absent from the body is to be present with the Lord (2 Cor. 5:8). Do you fear death, Christian? Do you worry about what you will leave behind? If God has ordained that He take you home, then it is good and right that it happens. Christ Himself will console you and comfort you. You will understand in the richest way how safe your loved ones are under His care and shepherding eye. You will be in the arms of your sovereign King and you will be basking in the full knowledge of absolute security. Your trust will be more solid than granite as you look into the eyes of your Savior and you will be assured of His ability to providentially provide for those you have left behind. There is no fear in love. Whate'er my God ordains is right. When the angels carry your soul to glory, it will be in God's perfect timing.

But here is the application at this point: if it is appointed for man once to die and then the judgment, if we can all be assured that God will indeed take us home one day- any day! maybe today! maybe tomorrow! then, we must put all our heart, mind, soul and strength into living for Christ now! To live is Christ!

For the sake of Christ, for the sake of your soul's reward, for the sake of those you love- live for Christ! Cast off your anger, cast off your lusts, cast off your moodiness, cast off your selfishness, cast of your vain-glory and live for Christ!

> Now He who has prepared us for this very thing is God, who also has given us the Spirit as a guarantee. So we are always confident, knowing that while we are at home in the body we

are absent from the Lord. For we walk by faith, not by sight. We are confident, yes, well pleased rather to be absent from the body and to be present with the Lord. THEREFORE! We make it our aim, whether present or absent, to be well pleasing to Him. For we must all appear before the judgement seat of Christ, that each one may receive the things done in the body, according to what he has done, whether good or bad (2 Cor. 5:5-10).

"Dying with Jesus, by death reckoned mine; Living with Jesus, a new life divine; Looking to Jesus till glory doth shine, Moment by moment, O Lord, I am thine."[12]

Determined To Remain

Our first point was that Paul was assured of deliverance. This was our first bookend, our first piece of bread of the sandwich, as it were. And we have moved down into the meat of the passage, the crux which is: to live is Christ to die is Gain. Paul knew, he has this mindset of assurance of not being ashamed because he held close to the gospel of Jesus Christ which allowed him to live for Christ in a way that he already viewed himself as dead.

But now we cap off this passage with our other bookend, our other instance of the mental word "know" in verse 25. But the context begins in verse 22:

> But if I live on in the flesh, this will mean fruit from my labor; yet what I shall choose I cannot tell. For I am hard-pressed between the two, having a desire to depart and be with Christ, which is far better. Nevertheless to remain in the flesh is more needful for you. And being confident of this, I KNOW that I shall remain and continue with you all for your progress and

---

[12] From the hymn "Moment by Moment" by Daniel W. Whittle, 1840-1901.

joy of faith, that your rejoicing for me may be more abundant in Jesus Christ by my coming to you again (Phil. 1:22-26, capitalization mine).

Our second bookend is that Paul was *determined to remain*. Many commentators believe that as Paul was previously uncertain whether he would be released, that, suddenly in these verses he comes to a kind of prophetic confidence that he will be released: "I know that I shall remain and continue with you all for your progress and joy of faith." I tend instead to agree with O'Brien in his commentary on Philippians that Paul was confident that if he remained it would be more profitable, but he was not absolutely certain what the future would hold.

Paul realized that to remain in the flesh is more needful for the churches. He was actually confident that it would be better at this point if his life is spared and if he postponed his full union with Christ in order to bear more fruit for Him by his life in the body. You see, Paul has weighed the pros and cons, as it were, and he has realized that it is more needful that he remain living. With that confidence, he knows that as far as he is concerned, he is determined to remain.

This is the beauty of the apostle's heart that had been set free in Christ. Though he longed to be with Christ, though he longed for release and rest and glory and holiness, he was nevertheless determined to remain. You see, though to die is gain for Paul, he was still determined to live for Christ. There is more work to be done. There is more labor to be accomplished for the cause of the kingdom. People are dependent on Paul. Yes, he is disposable in God's hands. But Paul realizes that he is called to serve Christ, to live for Christ, to the fullest extent possible. He sees that he can still do more, and he is determined to remain.

Perhaps there are some reading this book who are sick and frail. Or perhaps your mind and heart are absolutely strung out by life's circumstances and consequences. You might have some kind of chronic health condition, chronic pain, continual bouts of depression. Maybe you have been diagnosed with a mortal illness. Or perhaps you are getting older, and you feel it is time to coast into glory now. Whatever the case may be, the pains and heartaches and the tiredness of life has brought you to a place where you just want to ease off on pressing into Christ's kingdom, and just drift the rest of your time on this earth. Of course, you cannot do things the way you previously could, you do not have the same vigor you once did, and you might be in bed much of the time. But rather than give up and just coast into glory, have you not instead considered that you must remain for a while longer? Perhaps you have yet to perform your "magnum opus" for the Lord, your "great work" in your career as a pilgrim. It might not be according to what man views as a "great work", but if you determine to remain and live for the glory of God in the midst of your inabilities you might just come to know that the sweetest fruit of your life will be born in these last years of battle.

We cannot assume it is our time depart now. Though the gain of death for Christians is such a desire of ours because we will be present with the Lord, this is our time to live for Christ. There will be no other time in all of eternity where we can glorify Christ the way we can in this life. To glorify Him as we battle against sin, and to love Jesus and others while we are suffering, produces a sweet aroma in the nostrils of God that can only be created now, during this pilgrim life. Of course, it will waft on throughout eternity, but it can only be produced, it can only originate in this present life, amidst the evils of this world.

So it is that in many cases we must determine to remain. To live is Christ. We cannot bear this kind of fruit at any other time throughout the infinite recesses of eternity. Magnify Christ at every moment, with every breath, with every step, and let God take you to be with Him as you are *running* the race. You have to be running to cross the finish line. You cannot stop during the race and expect to finish well. Paul knew this. He knew he would not be ashamed were he to die there in Rome at that time. He knew rest and peace and joy awaited him. He knew it was good to be present with the Lord. But he determined to remain. He knew that he would continue on with the Philippians and the other churches because he had more fruit to bear from his labor. To live is

Christ. We bear fruit for Him as we cling to the gospel, as we meditate on the fact that we will be delivered on that Day.

But yes, indeed, to die is gain. I often hear people talk about how death is natural. It is just part of life, they say. And at many funerals, death is kind of accepted as this natural process of life for a human being. I can understand why people think that way. Especially when you are mourning, you want comfort over the idea of death, and you want to think your loved one passed on in a natural way. You want to think of death as something that is part of life. We live, we die- C'est la vie.

But, my friends, death was never meant to be part of the life God created. Death is actually unnatural. It has entered the world because of sin. Sin has perverted and twisted God's good design into something horrific. Yes, we all must die. But death is unnatural. Now this is especially so for the unbeliever. Death for them, for the non-Christian, is not only something that is against life and health and the joy of living, but death is a doorway to eternal suffering under the wrath of God. As the body shuts down, the soul slips away into eternal judgment, eternal shame, and everlasting agony in darkness and fire.

The wages of sin is death (Rom. 6:23). And death is not just a fading away into extinction. It is the beginning of eternal death for those who do not know Christ.

But the Bible says that death has no sting for the Christian (1 Cor. 15:55). Death, though unnatural, and though many Christians suffer as they die, and though Christians struggle as their bodies quit working; though Christians may grasp at life as they begin to fade and feel unnatural as their soul begins to leave their bodies, *there is no sting to it!* The blood of Christ shed for sinners has removed the sting of death and cured the Christian of its venom. In Christ, we are no longer children of wrath, but death for us is *gain*! Death is simply for us, a doorway. Though we many times experience suffering as we pass through this doorway, it nevertheless ushers us into eternal life where all sorrow, fear, and pain- all is taken away from us never to disturb us again. FOREVER!

Death is gain for the Christian. We need to think of how good it will be for us if we are Christians when we pass through death. We need to prepare ourselves to fight that final battle of struggling for life. But we need to desire to be with Christ. Everything we have ever known of true goodness in this life, every pleasure we have experienced that stems from love and righteousness, or even of enjoying the good things God has given us to enjoy- all these things will have a kind of fulfillment when we come to the fountain of life and goodness. Eternity with Christ will be going home. All you have ever known and felt about home as a good, safe, loving, restful, fulfilling place will be fulfilled in a completed and manifested fullness when we depart to be with Christ forever.

Therefore, like Paul, we are assured of deliverance. We will pass into glory when death comes. To live is Christ, but to die is gain. But then, also like Paul, until we know our time has come, we must determine to remain. For though to die is gain, to live… is CHRIST!

Chapter Four

Only let your conduct be worthy of the gospel of Christ, so that whether I come and see you or am absent, I may hear of your affairs, that you stand fast in one spirit, with one mind striving together for the faith of the gospel, and not in any way terrified by your adversaries, which is to them a proof of perdition, but to you of salvation, and that from God. For to you it has been granted on behalf of Christ, not only to believe in Him, but also to suffer for His sake, having the same conflict which you saw in me and now hear is in me –Philippians 1:27-30

The Bible contains what seems to me to be an endless amount of treasure to be discovered. There is always something to be mined from the Bible and to be feasted upon by the soul of the Christian. Over the course of the previous chapters we have found within this precious, ancient, God-breathed letter, gems and jewels contained within which point us to a certain *mindset* we are to have. What we see throughout these passages we are considering are different facets to the diamond of the Scriptural mindset which the Holy Spirit would have us to know and experience as Christians.

Our mental word in this last section of the first chapter of Philippians is contained in this phrase: "one mind", "that you stand fast in one spirit, with one mind". The Greek word translated "mind" here is actually the word for "soul", which is the inner self, the seat of the feelings, desires, affections, aversions.[13] Whereas the word for "spirit" here is almost syn-

---

[13] Joseph H. Thayer. *Thayer's Greek-English Lexicon of the New Testament* (Hendrickson Publishers, 2014), 677

onymous with the word for "soul", it means here the "state of mind"[14] or "inner life"[15]. So really, "spirit" and "mind" in the English are fairly synonymous in the Greek. It is that inner self, that frame of mind. One soul, one spirit: different angles on the same thing.

The Philippians are to be one in soul, one in their frame of mind. The Holy Spirit desires that the church be unified, that she be single-minded and together in the cause of Christ, together in the ways of Christ and in the message of Christ and His doctrine. Satan is the great divider, and his introduction of sin into the human race has absolutely fractured every aspect of our families and our society. It is God's plan for the church of Jesus Christ and through the church of Jesus Christ that we see unity restored in men, women, boys and girls.

Here in our passage, the mindset is for us to be one soul, one frame of mind with other Christians. We see three aspects to this unity: first, it must be worthy of the gospel, second, it must cause us to be together for the gospel, and finally, it grants us to suffer for the gospel.

Worthy of the Gospel

We read in Philippians 1:27: "Only let your conduct be worthy of the gospel of Christ, so that whether I come and see you or am absent, I may hear of your affairs, that you stand fast in one frame of mind with one soul striving together for the faith of the gospel." The word "worthy" speaks of the idea of having worthy weights in measurement scales. Something I saw occur often in the bush of Africa while I was on the mission field was the same thing that took place all throughout the ancient world. Often you would have people selling vegetables or fruit in the markets, and those selling the goods would have scales. On one side of the scale, they put the vegetables you are buying, and on the other side they put a weight. The weight must correspond to the market price- it has to

---

[14] Barbara Aland, Kurt Aland, Johannes Karavidopoulos, Carlo M. Martini, and Bruce M. Metzger. *The UBS Greek New Testament Reader's Edition with Textual Notes* (Deutsche Bibelgesellschaft, 2001), 711

[15] Warren C. Trenchard. *Complete Vocabulary Guide to the Greek New Testament Revised Edition* (Zondervan, 1998), 92

be *worthy* of the amount it is representing. So, what you have many times, (and this was the case in the ancient world) is that wicked business owners would place false weights or weights that were not worthy on one side of the scale. The result being that you would end up paying more than the vegetables or the goods you are purchasing were actually worth. As they say today, you would get "ripped off". So, when Paul says that the Philippians' conduct must by worthy of the gospel of Christ, he is saying their lives must match up to the weight of the gospel of Christ, they must correspond with its value.

Have you ever analyzed your own life like that? Do your actions, do your thoughts, do your priorities, does your love, does your financial commitment, does your labor, does it all match up in worthiness compared to the gospel of Jesus Christ? Now, of course, we know the gospel is invaluable. It is worth more than any of us could ever imagine. The gospel is really eternal and infinite in its ramifications. So how can our conduct ever be called *worthy* of it?

Well, in this case we are taking the etymology of this word a little too far. Let the idea of the weights in the scales help you, not hinder you. Paul is not saying our conduct will be matched to the actual worth of the gospel. But what he is saying is that our lives should match up with the gospel in such a way that is proper of a Christian man or woman, boy or girl living in this present evil age, battling against sin, and fighting the fight of faith. And yet, at the same time they are having this knowledge of Christ, having this gift of eternal life, having this mercy of the forgiveness of sins, and they have been set free from the bondage of the devil and the blindness of this world system of antichristian values.

To have our conduct worthy of *that* does not mean we will actually live in perfection, for that is truly the only thing that can come close to measuring up to the gospel's worth. It does mean we will act in such a way that is proper, that is according to the grace that has been given to us. We must not live in such a way that we disgrace the gospel, in other words. We must live up to the name of *Christian*. We should not conduct ourselves in a way that brings disrepute on the gospel or in a way that mars the message of the kingdom of God. We must not make the good news of Jesus Christ unclear to the world around us by the way we speak, the way we dress, or the way we entertain ourselves. There should not be a question as to what we are about when it really comes down to it.

"Did you know that Joe at work is a Christian?"

"Really? 20 years I have worked with that guy and I never even thought he was one of *those* people? Really? But he's just like me!" God forbid we should be talked about like that in the workplace!

No, there should be a matching up with the gospel in our conduct. Can this be the reason why Christians are so often made fun of in the marketplace? We claim big ideas: Heaven, Hell, sin, the existence of God, the Bible as the infallible word of God. But then, so often we act like we really do not believe any of it!

Here are two big areas where professing Christians in America continually fail in regards to their witness to the world and to family members: prayer and the Bible. If we believe what we believe about God and His power and His glory, then why are we not praying? Why are prayer meetings so often the least attended ministries of the church? Why are our prayer closets so often neglected day in and day out, if we believe the gospel of Christ? How many times do we choose an evening of television over an evening of private prayer and devotion?

And then there is the Bible. If we believe it is the word of God, why is it so distasteful to so many in the church today? Why are we so unfamiliar with it? Why have we not read through it ten or twenty times already? Why is it such a struggle to buckle down and meditate on the Scriptures? Is our conduct worthy of the gospel of Christ? We often see that the world mocks and despises Christians, not so much always because of the message we preach, but, because we preach the message, but we fail to live up to it.

Together for the Gospel

What is the main way Paul here in Philippians says we are to live lives worthy of the gospel of Christ? It is when we are as one mind, one spirit, and as one soul together for the gospel. Unity for the sake of the gospel. Unity in heart to spread the faith. Bonded together in love and like-mindedness in order to labor, strive, work, groan, sweat, and bleed for the sake of the faith of the gospel.

This is to be what we are unified in and what we are bonded together in: the fight, the battle, to win souls! If you are a member of a local church, why have you joined yourself to that body of believers? Is it go to the services and to be fed by the word of God? That is a good reason in and of itself. But why do you go to be fed by the preaching of the Bible? To help you through the difficulties and problems of life? Is it in order to encourage your soul? Do you attend church so that you can spend time with friends, with the family of God? Those are all decent enough reasons for going to a church service.

However, if that is all, or if all the reasons we just mentioned are all *primary*, then, we are missing it! Paul starts off this passage by saying "Only". "Only let your conduct be worthy". In the Greek it is saying: "Just one thing!"[16] Paul is declaring, "There's just one thing I want you people to do! Live your lives in worthiness to the gospel by striving in one soul for the spread of the Kingdom of God!"

If you think the church is simply a vehicle for you to be edified, for you to have your path set straight (and it is those things for us all!)- if that is all the church is for you, you are missing out on the one thing Paul is trying to get across in this passage! In fact, you are not in the same frame of mind that many believers are trying to maintain: a striving for the faith of the gospel. The English Standard Version here reads: "Striving side by side for the faith of the gospel." We need to be working together, my

---

[16] Peter T. O'Brien. *The Epistle to the Philippians, A Commentary on the Greek Text* (William B. Eerdmans Publishing Company, The Paternoster Press, 1991), 145

friends. Working! Yes, the Lord's Day is a day of rest, and time to recharging our souls. But the Lord's Day is also meant to get us on track for the callings we have in laboring for the cause of Jesus Christ.

We must be about our Father's business if we are to profess the name of Christ. Yet, not only is it paramount that we be working for the spread of the kingdom, the emphasis here is that we do it side by side. Unified! As one soul! Think of the analogy of the body. How does the body function? Is any part of the body concerned with itself? Concerned about its own recognition? Worried about how much credit it gets? Are our individual body parts concerned about standing out in relationship to the other members? Do they desire to promote their own way? Are members of our bodies greedy to grab resources from other parts of the body? No one can live if any of its appendages or organs or cells act in that way! What is that actually called when a member acts in those ways? It is called *cancer*.

What needs to be done in the church? Do it. *You* do it. What ministries do you think the church lacks? *You* think about starting it. Talk to your elders about it, of course, but *you* pray about starting up the needed ministry. Are you unable to go to the weekly prayer meeting? Start a prayer meeting in your own home some other night of the week, or some morning of the week perhaps. Do you see some enterprise which lacks laborers? Get involved.

Make sure you do not fall into the mistake of thinking that your pastors will have some special premonition from God and will ask you to do some kind of ministry if you are called to it. Have you ever thought that way? You have decided not to take any step forward in being involved in something unless the pastor tells you to do it. Not that you do not ask the pastors in your church about your ideas or your desires. There is still a place for the leading officers of the church in these issues. But, if you honestly feel like doing something for the Lord and you have been waiting for one of your elders to identify you, do not be shy! Go and talk to them about your desires for the Christ.

All that to say, we should not shut up ourselves within our own families, having our own plans that do not contain any thoughts towards the extension of the mission of Jesus Christ to the world. Do you go to your church for fellowship? Good. But be sure to fellowship in such a way that you are striving side by side with other believers for the faith of the gospel. Maybe you are engaging at some point on a Sunday in a conversation with another brother about the homeless who are in your area. "Boy, it has been getting out of hand!" you exclaim. Possibly you could consider sitting down with that brother and pray about this issue. Is there a need for some kind of homeless ministry at your church? How does that start? How does that happen? What do *you* do? Meet for prayer about it at the very least!

Or perhaps you are talking to another sister about how awful it is that abortion is legal in this country. Well, can you begin asking each other how you can make a difference? You might suggest that you and your friend arrange to collect items for the local pregnancy center. Meet together to pray for the Supreme Court that has power to pass laws to protect the unborn. You can gather with other sisters and pray for couples who are trying to adopt.

You might be a young person going to university and you have been talking with another person about how crazy the party scene is on campus. How can you make a difference? How can you strive together for the faith of the gospel there? Start a Christian club on campus? Start a Bible study? Start singling out other students to try to get to know them and to be a witness to them? Start praying together at the very least!

What does it mean to strive side by side in the church of Jesus Christ? What if this coming Sunday you actually start talking to another member in the congregation about this. How can you strive more for the kingdom of God? Brainstorm together about possible ideas. After the sermon has been preached, what do you do after the service? Do you talk about the sermon with anyone else? Do you seek to build more upon it? Together? As One soul?

Now at this point we need to discuss something about the doctrine of vocation. According to this Reformed doctrine, each of us is serving Christ, glorifying Christ, and providing means for the gospel to advance through our station and calling in life. Our jobs are what we are called to and it is not necessary to be involved in a Christian-labeled ministry to be used by God, in other words. If we neglect our vocations in life by isolating ourselves from the world in the sense of only doing *Christian* work, only doing so called "ministries", or thinking that godly labors consist only in doing something as an outreach of the church or as some kind of church-sponsored program- then we are forsaking our calling in life. Each of us has been called to be Christians *in the midst* of society in each of our jobs and vocations. We do not necessarily want our church buildings to have every day filled with church ministries and activities throughout the week and that we end up like a Christian ghetto, neglecting our witness to the world and in our God-given vocations.

Now, let me also say something regarding doing too much. There is a danger in biting off more than we can chew, of over committing ourselves. We can do it so much so that in the end we really accomplish nothing for the Lord. Furthermore, many of us have a God-given priority to take care of and nourish our families. Though throughout church history, many great saints have accomplished amazing things for Christ, in many cases they have pursued laboring for the Lord at the expense of their families. Though the ends of these labors have been glorious and have born much fruit to the glory of God, they nonetheless do not justify many of the means these great men and women of God have taken up to accomplish these incredible works while they neglected their spouses and their children in the process.

Though we might accomplish less in the immediate time by tending to our loved ones as a priority, the conviction of this writer is that ultimately the fruit will be more solid and more lasting if we take the wisdom and the love to order our lives rightly according to Biblical principles. Though we have zeal for the gospel of Christ, we must not taint it by leaving our children in the dust to fend for themselves in the face of this world's pressures and cruelty because mom and dad felt a calling to serve the Lord in this or that ministry.

Also, there is the danger of over-extending ourselves. If you feel called to serve Christ in some way, please count the cost before you seek to do it. Here, I am only speaking to the overly zealous who want to do all they can for Christ, but who many times fail to have the wisdom as to how best to accomplish tasks for the Lord. Their eye of faith is bigger than their belly of ability, in other words. Many have been wracked with physical illness or depression because their bodies and their minds cannot keep up with the pace they set in doing the Lord's work.

But at the same time, I cannot say Paul the apostle was in sin for buffeting his body to keep it subjected to the ways and cause of Christ. Meaning this: he sacrificed all to glorify God and to fight against sin. (Now, Paul did not have a wife or children, we must note). I also cannot say any of the martyrs of 16th and 17th century Great Britain were in sin for risking their lives for the gospel of Jesus Christ, or for putting their families on the line by allowing themselves to be burned at the stake for the sake of God's word. They often did so when they were the only bread winner for the wife and children they left behind. I cannot say that Adonirum Judson and John Paton were in sin for bringing their lives into danger for the sake of the gospel of Jesus Christ! I cannot say C.H. Spurgeon was in the wrong for accomplishing so much for Christ, though I have my doubts about the treatment and care he gave to his own body and constitution in his zeal for ministry.

My point in all this is that striving for the gospel means blood, sweat and tears! It means plodding along when the path is difficult. It means going against the grain. It means doing things when other people mock and doubt and discourage you! Yes, but in each of our own individual callings, we must weigh what it means to be a good steward of our bodies and of our families. We must seek to follow Christ and to strive for the faith of the gospel and to not shrink from what God is calling us to do. However, we must be careful to know what it is we have been called to, what responsibilities God has given us to take care of and nourish others versus what we are called to sacrifice and put on the altar before God for the cause of the kingdom.

Just one thing! Paul would say. Conduct yourselves worthy of the gospel, so much so that you strive together, side by side, for the work of Christ. If all of us in the church have this frame of mind, to be bent towards the cause of the kingdom, then we will be one soul. And then, the world cannot laugh at us for the same reasons it has done so in the past.

Someone at this point might be picking out that this chapter is largely an imperative. This is what the text is saying. But you see, embedded within the DO THIS! Within the "Only let your conduct be worthy". Contained in the midst of the imperative there is the indicative of what Christ has done for us: "the gospel of Christ". None of this can be worked up in a vacuum. The Philippians mindset is in the context of the New Testament: the declaration of who Christ is and what He has done for the church.

When we see in our mind's eye the wounds and the scars Christ was marked with due to Him wrestling our souls from Hell, how can we not be moved to serve such a savior with our very lives? When we think upon all that Christ has won for us, accomplished for us, and given to us because of His work on the cross which was sealed with approval and victory by His resurrection from the dead, how can we not die to all worldly ambitions and designs and devote our strength to the cause of the gospel?

Alas! And did my Saviour bleed, and did my Sovereign die!/ Would he devote that sacred head for such a worm as I!

Was it for crimes that I had done He groaned upon the tree!/ Amazing pity! Grace unknown! And love beyond degree!

Well might the sun in darkness hide, and shut his glories in/ When Christ, the mighty maker died, for man the creature's sin.

Thus might I hide my blushing face While his dear cross appears/ Dissolve my heart in thankfulness, and melt mine eyes in tears.

But drops of grief can ne'er repay the debt of love I owe;/ Here, Lord, I give myself away, 'Tis all that I can do.[17]

Only let your conduct be *worthy of the gospel of Christ*…. Stand fast in one spirit, with one mind striving together *for the faith of the gospel*. Do not wander away from the gospel, from the doctrine, or from the truth of what Christ has done for sinners as you seek to "do" for Him. Let the truth of His extravagant love and sacrifice fill your heart and soul. Let it all empower you with love and compassion and pour into you a full heart that can only but overflow to those around you. We find no power or hope in drawing water from an empty well. Go to the gospel. Go to the cross. Go to Christ and fill your cup. You cannot serve and strive without love. To labor and bleed without compassion is futile. Praying and preaching without joy and hope and peace is only a mirage of spiritual life and vitality. We cannot strive side by side with others unless we know something of sweet fellowship with Jesus, because otherwise we will only sap the strength from other saints in the process.

Granted to Suffer for the Gospel

We are to be one spirit and one mind in striving for the gospel. And we are to do so in such a way that we understand we have been granted to suffer for the gospel. A dried and cracked well of a Christian will not be able to endure sufferings for the kingdom of God.

We read in verses 28-30:

> And not in any way terrified by your adversaries, which is to them a proof of perdition, but to you of salvation, and that from God. For to you it has been granted on behalf of Christ, not only to believe in Him, but also to suffer for His sake, having the same conflict which you saw in me and now hear is in me.

---
[17] From the Old Hymn by Isaac Watts, 1707

The Greek word for terrified in these verses, *pturomenoi*, is only found here in the Greek New Testament. O'Brien in his commentary translates this as "in no way letting your opponents intimidate you". He points out this word for terrified carries with it the idea of an uncontrollable stampede of startled horses.[18] The enemies of the gospel were trying to intimidate the Philippians with threats of and with actual occurrences of persecution. Paul tells them not to be intimidated. Do not get hysterical about threats and the news you hear, or in thinking about the things that have already happened to you. Stand firm in one spirit, with one mind. God has not only given you the grace to believe in Christ for salvation, but God has given you the grace you need to endure suffering.

Did you catch that? This is absolutely encouraging considering the context we live in today. Do not break ranks, church! Resist the urge to crumble under the pressure of an anti-Christian world system. God has granted you what you need to suffer for His gospel. That means even in the growing anxieties of all the "what ifs", God has given you grace. We are called to suffer, but Christ does not leave us to go through the difficulties alone.

The age-old story of the two seeds in the Bible is that the seed of the serpent will be trying to intimidate and eradicate the seed of the woman throughout history. But the plans of the seed of the serpent will never succeed because the Seed of Eve has already crushed his head![19] Why is there so much intimidation and persecution and threatening and abuse against the church throughout history? Why is religious freedom becoming narrower and narrower today? Because the devil and the world are scared stiff of the coming judgment deep down within their souls and they hate the gospel! They want no reminders of the God they are at enmity against. Satan is on borrowed time and he is raging mad because he is defeated and knows he is going to burn under the wrath of Almighty God for all eternity.

---

[18] Peter T. O'Brien. *The Epistle to the Philippians, A Commentary on the Greek Text* (William B. Eerdmans Publishing Company, The Paternoster Press, 1991), 152

[19] Genesis 3:15

Have you ever seen a line of ants crawling on the ground? Perhaps you did this as a child. What happens when you stomp on that line of ants crawling on the concrete? The ants go crazy and start speeding all over the place, they are frantic and might even crawl up your leg and bite you. This is really what is going on in the world today. Satan and his seed are crushed ants scurrying about like mad, trying to shut up the church!

Do not be intimidated by that. It is actually a proof of their perdition. Psalm 2:1-6 reads,

> Why do the nations rage, and the people plot a vain thing? The kings of the earth set themselves, and the rulers take counsel together, Against the LORD and against His Messiah, saying, Let us break their bonds in pieces and cast away their cords from us. He who sits in the heavens shall laugh; The LORD shall hold them in derision. Then He shall speak to them in His wrath, and distress them in His deep displeasure; Yet I have set My King on my holy hill of Zion.

The Philippians were under constant threat of persecution, and indeed they had experienced a degree of actual persecution. Paul tells them not to freak out like startled horses and to run every which way for some kind of comfort or relief. The very fact that animosity grows towards the church in our world and that we feel pressure building up against us is a proof that the world is headed for judgment. They are raging ants, going crazy, trying to stop any reminder of the wrath of the God they hate against the sin that they love so dearly.

But it is at the same time proof and reminder to us that we are indeed God's children, that our salvation is real, and that we are not citizens of this world. We can talk all day long about the news and current events and ring the alarm bell, as it were. But what I want to know is how am I to *live* in the midst of this crooked and perverse generation? How do we walk with God in these present times? Of course, we pray against the tide of evil. That is one aspect of walking with God. But what else?

We are not to be terrified by the enemies of the church. God has not only given us the grace we need to have faith in Christ for salvation, but He has graciously granted us the ability to suffer for the sake of Christ. Moises Silva interprets these verses by paraphrasing them as Paul saying this:

> The conflicts that you are experiencing may appear frightening and thus threaten to discourage you, but you cannot allow that to happen. Perhaps you are tempted to interpret these conflicts as a bad omen, as though God is displeased with you and intends to destroy you. But that is exactly wrong. You must interpret what is happening as evidence of God's design to save you! Why? Because suffering is the way to glory, God's gift of salvation for his children.[20]

Have you ever looked at someone from church history, like the apostle Paul, and thought, "I know he suffered much, but if I had his faith and the amount of grace he had, I feel like I would be able to face suffering so much easier." Well, we must first of all admit that things were not exactly easy for Paul. And yet, he did have great grace in his life. He understood so much of what Christ had done for him. It was only because of his deep Biblical, Holy Spirit- saturated mindset that he was able to endure so much for the cause of the gospel.

And he writes here to the Philippians, "Having the same conflict which you saw in me and now hear is in me." Paul is telling them, in so many words, that they are in the same boat as he is in. They have the same savior as Paul. *We*, 21st century Christians, have the same savior as Paul! Please do not think I am saying any of us can be as great as Paul the apostle! But we have the same conflict, we have the same God graciously granting us faith in Christ and granting us the grace to suffer for Him. We experience this each in our own callings and according to God's decree regarding our own lives.

---

[20] Moises Silva. *Philippians, Baker Exegetical Commentary on the New Testament* (Baker Academic, 2005), 83

And if you look around you in your local church, each of your brothers and sisters in Christ have the same conflict you have. Each of us are enduring trials, afflictions, fighting against sin, having to deal with tragic circumstances- *suffering*! We can encourage each other as one soul, knowing that we all have the same conflict, we have the same gift of being conformed into the image of Christ. Often times it is through the means of suffering.

Do you wonder why things just seem to keep piling up? "Why is it so much has been going wrong in my life?" you might ask. "Is God mad at me? Am I cursed?" No! You are being *saved*! And it hurts, yes! But God will complete the work He started in you, as we read in chapter one. It is all working for good. There is nothing needful that he withholds, as John Newton once said. We are not in a raging sea alone, destined to break apart in the waves. Jesus Christ, our Captain, holds the helm and will steer the vessel through all the waves and billows as deep calls unto deep.

We are not alone. We have each other as Christians. We have the example and the writings of the apostles. We have Christ! We are to have one soul, one mind. Sailing along, side by side, diffusing the fragrance of Christ wherever we go, sowing seeds, watering seeds, building up the church, giving ourselves as living sacrifices, not counting our lives dear to ourselves, loving to the very end. All because we have been given faith in the gospel of Christ. All because His side was rent, His hands and feet pierced, his brow crowned with thorns. All because our dear savior bled and died for us.

Chapter Five

Therefore if there is any consolation in Christ, if any comfort of love, if any fellowship of the Spirit, if any affection and mercy, fulfill my joy by being likeminded, having the same love, being of one accord, of one mind. Let nothing be done through selfish ambition or conceit, but in lowliness of mind let each esteem others better than himself. Let each of you look out not only for his own interests, but also for the interests of others. Let this mind be in you which was also in Christ Jesus, who, being in the form of God, did not consider it robbery to be equal with God, but made Himself of no reputation, taking the form of a bond-servant, and coming in the likeness of men. And being found in appearance as a man, He humbled Himself and became obedient to the point of death, even the death of the cross. Therefore God also has highly exalted Him and given Him the name which is above every name, that at the name of Jesus every knee should bow, of those in heaven, and of those on earth, and of those under the earth, and that every tongue should confess that Jesus Christ is Lord, to the glory of God the Father. -Philippians 2:1-11

If you have ever had a mentor in your life, or desired that someone be your mentor, you know that they do not just have good information to teach you. In a mentor/mentee relationship, the disciple is seeking to get to a place where he not only acts like his teacher, but *thinks* like his teacher. In this chapter, Paul opens up for us the way to think the way the greatest Master in the history of the world thought.

This chapter flows directly out of our last study of the mindsets of 1:27-30. The togetherness, or the unity we saw Paul urge the Philippians toward when he says in 1:27, "that you stand fast in one spirit, with one mind, striving together for the faith of the gospel"- this focus on unity of mind and unity of mindset flows directly into chapter 2. Paul says in this passage: "fulfill my joy by being likeminded, having the same love, being of one accord, of one mind." This whole section of the mindset that Paul is exhorting the Philippians towards comes to a crescendo in verse 5 and following where he wrote: "let this mind be in you which was also in Christ Jesus…"

Indeed, the passage we are considering in chapter 2 is the heart, the core of the Philippians mindset. This is really the marrow of the book of Philippians. This is the center of the Christian life, and it centers on the Lord Jesus Christ. This is the essence of Christian love. This is where the second greatest commandment (To love your neighbor as yourself) finds its anchor in the love of God: God's love for us and in turn, us loving Him. It is loving God with all our heart, *mind*, soul and strength through adorning ourselves with the very mind of Jesus Christ.

The New Dictionary of Biblical Theology says this: "Christian love can be understood, and best practiced, only when it is seen to be a reflection of God's love in its varied dimensions."[21] In consideration of this truth we recognize that this passage is a feast of Christian love. It is a banquet where we can immerse ourselves in the Biblical mindset Christ has called us to clothe ourselves with as His image bearers.

We see here in this passage four divisions or aspects to this mindset. In verse 1 we see the Beauty of Christian love. In verse 2 we see the Unity of Christian love. In verses 3- 4 we see the Humility of Christian love. And in verses 5-8 we see the Humility of Christ's love.

The Beauty of Christian Love

"Therefore if there is any consolation in Christ, if any comfort of love, if any fellowship of the Spirit, if any affection and mercy…"

Paul is making an appeal here for the Philippians to be unified in their mindset (to be like-minded) by him saying "*If* there" is any love or encouragement or spiritual fellowship or affection or mercy in the church

---

[21] T. Desmond Alexander and Brian S. Rosner, eds. *New Dictionary of Biblical Theology* (Inter-Varsity Press, 2000), 649

of Jesus Christ, then fulfill my joy by being likeminded. Even though he is speaking in verse 1 in a kind of appeal from the negative, he nevertheless is, at the same time, painting before the Philippians a positive picture of the beauty of Christian love.

Here in verse 1 Paul lists off some of the virtues of Christian unity. He describes what the body of Christ should be looking like, and what it should be reflecting out to the world around them. These are virtues of body life that should be reverberating throughout our local church buildings as we gather on the Lord's Day. These are aspects of Christian love that should be pulsating in our care for one another, in our concern for one another, in our interest in one another, in our respect for one another, in our giving, in our sacrificing, in our patience with others and in our bearing the burdens of others.

Consolation in Christ. This could be called *encouragement* in Christ. This is really a virtue of the church that we find when we, as individual believers take up the means of grace. Christians should be finding nourishment, sustenance, and encouragement in the Lord Jesus Christ. If you come to a group of professing Christians who gather together on a Sunday and none of the people there are knowing experientially the encouragement found in the gospel of the Lord Jesus Christ and in the fellowship of the Son of God- if none of those professing the name of Christ and who congregate together for a church service know the experience of being guided by the Holy Scriptures and they do not know what it is to exercise an eagerness to point others to the Lord Jesus Christ, then you really do not have a *church* which is coming together at all.

Gathering together as believers on a Lord's Day is done in order to find consolation in Jesus Christ! We come to be encouraged in the worship, in the service of, and in the knowledge of our Savior! If you come to the church service for other reasons than that, and if that is not your main goal in coming to church and in professing the name of Christ, then we might assume you are fairly miserable when you attend a worship service. Why else would you spend your Sunday coming into a building and listening to a man speak to you for an hour? Why else would you sit through singing Christian hymns and songs? Afterall, the songs sung in churches are not pop songs from platinum record sales! No, Christians come to church gatherings in order to worship God and to receive consolation in Christ Jesus.

The beauty of love that marks the church is her desire for the lover of her soul: Jesus! We come to services on a Sunday after stacking up a bank-load of sins during the week, and thus we need to find consolation in the gospel of Jesus Christ. We come to find encouragement in the One who ever lives to make intercession between God and man, the One in whom wrath and mercy meet and in whom our sins are washed away in the blood of His suffering which He endured 2,000 years ago in a historical moment in space and time.

Christian love flows from the cross of Jesus Christ. It flows from the great high priest, the Son of God who stands interceding for His children. It is His love we are unable to be separated from. No stain too deep, no scar too ugly, no sin too heinous- "Jesus ready stands to save"- and Jesus ready stands for the Christian as the One to whom we can confess our sins to again and again. We can realize afresh and anew by the encouragement of Christ that we have been justified through His cross work on behalf of sinners.

As we receive consolation, we are filled with thanksgiving and the power and desire to spend and to be spent for the glory of God. This is what the church is all about: The beauty of Christian love. Consolation in Christ.

Then the apostle says: "if any comfort of love". We are not only comforted by the love Christ has for those He died for, but we are comforted by the love the body of Christ has for itself. This is many times the reason that gets people out of a bed of despair and to come and seek some kind of truth in the local church. They desire comfort of love.

Who does not desire that? Is not this the desire of all who seek out pleasures in all kinds of things and in all kinds of relationships, and who abuse substances and look for answers in different religions and cults and the like? No one really does not want to be loved. If they say such things, it is actually out of a warped love for themselves. Why do people take their own lives? They are looking for an escape from the pain. They want comfort of love.

Christians know that the only true love that is not self-destructing and that is not harmful to them and to others is a love that loves Christ supreme. If you are a Christian, of course, you also are seeking comfort of love when you go to church. But you know it is found in Christ and His word. It is found in His gospel and in His people who reflect His image into your life. We find true comfort when we are encouraged in Christ, or when a brother or sister is used as the hands, the feet, or the ears or mouth of our great Shepherd, Jesus Christ.

Comfort of love in the church bears the burdens of others with the patience and hope of Christ. Comfort of love gently pushes another believer towards repentance, towards godliness, towards joyfulness. Comfort of love covers a multitude of sins; it forgives 70 times 70, and it repents again and again. Comfort of love also gets back up again and again to fight for truth, to fight for love, to seek out the stragglers and the wanderers. This is the beauty of Christian love: there is comfort of love.

There is also "fellowship of the Spirit". O'Brien notes this phrase means "Participation in the Spirit"[22]. In a church where Christian love is pulsating, the members of Christ's body know experientially fellowship with the Holy Spirit. He manifests Himself in quickening them to pray, in guiding the church in their prayers, and in urging them to pray. The Holy Spirit is with them as the Scriptures are illuminated in their minds and hearts while they take up the means of grace. He falls upon them in joy and heart-felt love for God as they sing songs, hymns and spiritual songs. He fills believers' hearts with conviction, with desire for Christ, with love for the church, and with a longing for heaven's realities as the Word of God is preached. The saints of God know the fellowship of the

---

[22] Peter T. O'Brien. *The Epistle to the Philippians, A Commentary on the Greek Text* (Wm. B. Eerdmans Publishing Co., 1991), 172

Spirit, and this spills out into the church as the beauty of Christian love, while the church is filled with the Spirit of Jesus Christ.

And finally, there is beauty in the affection and mercy found amongst God's people. The world can offer many cliques and clubs and groups of like-minded people. There might even be affection found within these groups. Often, unfortunately, it is affection that is misguided and harmful to the soul. Groups in which love is free and all are welcomed to engage in fornication can perhaps feed a longing for affection and love, but it becomes a bitter poison in the end that destroys the soul.

The New Testament speaks of the church as a place where affection and mercy should be prominent. It is the affection of caring for one another, not the affection of illicit behaviors. It is the mercy of being forgiving and seeking to restore, not the mercy of being welcomed into a gang or a clique from which you previously felt ostracized.

Colossians 3:12-13 says,

> Therefore as the elect of God, holy and beloved, put on tender mercies, kindness, humility, meekness, longsuffering: bearing with one another, and forgiving one another, if anyone has a complaint against another; even as Christ forgave you, so you also must do.

The church is a place of affection and mercy because it is a place where sinners have found affection and mercy from God. You cannot truly believe and know that God loved you so much that He sent His Son to die for you if you are not in turn filled with affection and mercy towards others in the body of Christ. We read in 1 John 5:10, 11, "He who loves his brother abides in the light, and there is no cause for stumbling in him. But he who hates his brother is in darkness and walks in darkness, and does not know where he is going, because the darkness has blinded his eyes."

The Unity of Christian Love

Paul is painting a picture in Philippians of the beauty of Christian love, but he is doing it as an appeal to the Unity of Christian love: "Fulfill my joy by being likeminded, having the same love, being of one accord, of one mind." We are to be unified in Christian love. We are to have the same mindset together as God's children. We learn about the mindset we are to have through Scripture and through the preaching of God's Word.

Have you ever felt disjointed from the rest of the church? Do you ever feel alone even when you are around so many people? When you first entered your own local church, after the service ended, did you feel discouraged and want to just get up and leave because it looked like everyone else had someone to talk to? After a church service, does it seem like everyone is in a group talking, and you are just sitting there twiddling your thumbs feeling awkward? Many of us have been there before. In fact, we could safely say most of us have been in that place at one time or another.

Let me pose a question: do you love the Lord Jesus Christ? Do you come to church because you want more of Him? Do you desire to live for His glory and to be used by Him? Many people who might feel alone during or after a church service would say yes to these questions. Paul would plead with you- not only with the person feeling alone- but with all Christians: if in Christ there is encouragement, and if in the church there should be affection and mercy and fellowship in the Spirit and comfort of love, then, he would say, fulfill my joy by being like-minded. Have the same love, be of the same mind.

Are you shy and alone, or are you feeling separated from the rest of the body? Seek to be like Christ! He has suffered and bled and risen from the dead for you! Can you therefore, in light of all that Jesus has done for you, lay your body on the altar, and offer it as a spiritual sacrifice, and try and try again? Can you seek to get up out of your seat in the main hall after worship and introduce yourself to others? Can you seek to find out others and join in their fellowship? Perhaps you might look for someone else who looks like they are feeling just like you, and you can go seek to encourage them in Christ.

Jesus Christ came to seek and to save that which was lost. Can we emulate the same kind of mindset? Seeking to comfort others in love? Not just our friends whom we know very well and talk to every Sunday, but those on the other side of the church hall or those who might leave quickly after service because they feel awkward.

The point is: to have this *one* mind Paul is talking about. When churches falter here, it opens up a place for the devil to cause splits and factions. If we are all unified in this spirit of Christian love, then Christ will be magnified, the body will be edified, and Satan will flee the church!

And how is it we follow the mind of Christ? How do we know like-mindedness? How can we experience a joining with others in the church? It is when we are all seeking to meditate on the word of God. It is when we are all worshiping God during a sermon being preached by praying the message into our hearts and taking captive our thoughts to the obedience of Christ.

Maybe you feel disjointed from some in the church because the word of Christ is not dwelling within you richly. The preaching of the Word is the central part of the worship service for a reason. Does your heart reverberate with the Psalmist when he says,

> Oh, how I love Your law! It is my meditation all the day. You, through Your commandments, make me wiser than my enemies; for they are ever with me. I have more understanding than all my teachers, for your testimonies are my meditation. I understand more than the ancients, because I keep your precepts. I have restrained my feet from every evil way, that I may keep your Word. I have not departed from your judgments, For You Yourself have taught me. How sweet are Your words to my taste, Sweeter than honey to my mouth! Through your precepts I get understanding; Therefore I hate every false way (Ps. 119:97-104).

We will falter in the Philippians mindset, over and over again. The only way to bring our hearts and minds closer in line with the mind of Christ is to meditate over and over again on the words of the Holy Spirit in Scripture.

The Humility of Christian Love

Again, this is the core section of the Philippians mindset: the unity of Christian love. The Unity of mind we are to have is really every aspect to the Philippians mindset we have been seeing in this inspired letter. Our passage in this chapter is kind of a centralizing text, a kind of gathering together of all Paul has been trying to say.

There is the beauty of Christian love and we are to have unity in that kind of mindset. But the marrow of this mindset is found in the humility of Christian love: "Let nothing be done through selfish ambition or conceit, but in lowliness of mind let each esteem others better than himself. Let each of you look out not only for his own interests, but also for the interests of others." Sinclair Ferguson notes that "when Augustine was asked to list the central principles of the Christian life he replied, 'First humility; second humility; third, humility.'"[23]

Something to consider here, when analyzing your own goals in life: is your life oriented on getting somewhere? Are you trying to be someone or get something in life? Do you desire to be in that position at work, or be an officer in the church maybe? Do you picture yourself as being all you can be when you arrive at a certain place in life or as achieving certain things?

Or is your life oriented not on where you want to be, but is it oriented on the moment- right now? Do you think, instead: how can I this very moment serve someone? How can I give myself to edify and bless others? When you are at work, is it: how can I get to the top? Or is it, how can I do a good job with what has been placed before me right now? Do you

---

[23] Sinclair B Ferguson. *Let's Study Philippians* (Banner of Truth Trust, 1997), 42

interact with other Christians with perhaps the subconscious mentality of: how will this benefit me in the future? Or do you interact with other Christians with perhaps the subconscious mentality of: how can I do good to this sister right now?

Do you walk past the hurting brother at church in order to meet up with a group of your friends out on the patio? Furthermore, if you are one who sees that tables need to be cleaned in the fellowship hall or trash that needs to be taken out- why do you take care of those needs? Is it to be seen and noticed, or do you not care and just want to clean dirt for the glory of Christ alone?

As we consider this passage on the humility of Christian love, we need to be careful that we do not try to don this mindset with a concern for others to notice it about us. The Philippians mindset entails: I do not care what becomes of my service for Christ, I just want to love Jesus and love people because I have been saved from an eternity of Hell and it is the least I can do.

Humility is something that is always trying to elude us. Our innate pride makes holding onto humility like trying to hold a wet bar of soap. Every time we squeeze, it squirts out of our grasp. This is why we need to come over and over again to Scripture.

Paul says, "Let nothing be done through selfish ambition or conceit." The word here translated "selfish ambition" is the Greek word *Eritheian*. Kittel says this word speaks of the "attitude of self-seekers, harlots, etc., i .e., those who demeaning themselves and their cause, are busy and active in their own interests, seeking their own gain or advantage… This is the attitude of those who procure office by illegal manipulation."[24]

Kenodoxian, the Greek word translated "conceit", means: boasting, vainglory, talking big, trying to establish an unfounded opinion. Immediately, if you have been through such a thing, your mind should run to the causes of church splits. This is the heart of all inter-church contentions. This is where wolves rise up from among us. This is where the

---

[24] Gerhard Kittel, ed. *Theological Dictionary of the New Testament, vol. II* (Wm. B. Eerdmans Publishing Co., 1964), 660

devil drives his wedge and gains his beach head in the church of Jesus Christ: through those who seek selfish ambition and through those who are conceited.

This is the absolute opposite of Christian love and of the humility we are called to in Jesus. This is the complete opposite attitude of those who have been redeemed from a Hell they deserve. It is the complete opposite of those who are called to lead the church as well. Pastors and overseers of the flock of Christ must not be seeking their own gain or advantage. They must not be busy and active in promoting their own interests, seeking office by illegal manipulation.

The man or the woman who gets hold of a cause (albeit in the name of Christ) and digs in in order to die on that hill, no matter who they take out, no matter what the casualty- that person carries in their character a sure way for churches to splinter and fragment in division and animosity towards one another. O, the shame that so many have brought to the name of Christ before the eyes of the watching world by their selfish ambition- by their conceit! O, the countless pastors and church leaders and would-be leaders in the church that have strong-armed their own way into gaining advantage and in seeking to control things for their own promotion!

The One (the ONLY ONE!) who has any kind of claim to gain his own advantage is KING Jesus, and He did not live in such a way, no not at all. He came to give His life as a ransom for many. He came to wash His disciples' feet on the night of his betrayal. He came to die on a cross, pierced through as a criminal for crimes He was never even associated with in the least.

Do you follow this King? Then clothe yourself with the humility and the kindness of Christ. Clothe yourself in the love of Jesus. Do not be concerned only with your own interests. Seek out the good of other people's interests. Seek to have them elevated. Seek to have others exalted before you. Not because you want to be above them in the end when the rewards are dealt out, but because you truly esteem them as better than yourself.

Do you think you are better than the brother or sister in church you feel displays a lack of quality, a lack of godliness, or a rudeness or a shortcoming in graces? Do you feel you are better than a brother who you think does very little for the kingdom of God, while you yourself are maybe an officer in the church or part of the Sunday school ministry perhaps?

Do we really know what God is doing with His other servants? Can we make such a claim? Can we honestly position ourselves in our thoughts in front of and above other sinners saved by the grace of God just as we have been? Do we know from what point they started their road of sanctification? Do we know what they dealt with as a child? Do we know the abuse they encountered, the disappointments, the difficulty they had at school- not due to any lack of effort on their part? Do we know what they will go through in the future and what God might be preparing them for? Do we wish to go through the same trials God might have in store for them?

After reading all that, are you thinking that *you* are the one who is the victim here? Are you thinking that *you* are the one that *others* should think of more highly than themselves? If you think that then you are missing the point. All Christians have a great deal to learn and to grow in the ways of the Lord Jesus Christ. None of us are where we might think we are on the road of sanctification. Most of us are no doubt far below the mark that we imagine ourselves to have reached.

What we need to do is to let our lives flow out as a humble sacrifice for the cause of Christ, in the little things- yes in the little things! We do that before we attempt the great things. Do not condemn the one for whom Christ died. Do not write him or her off in your mind as beyond the scope of grace and Christian love.

Let love flow down and waters bound
Wherever you hear the gospel sound
Let Christian love and peace abound
Wherever gospel truths are found

It is our pride which clings so tightly to our own reputation! Do you believe you are being taken advantage of? Do you rehearse stepping into the situation and chewing someone out for the way they have tried to manipulate you and use you? Now, we realize we need to take care of ourselves and protect ourselves in a way that is good stewardship of our character and of our family's livelihood. But do you remember what Jesus said?

> You have heard that it was said, "An eye for and eye and a tooth for a tooth.' But I tell you not to resist an evil person. But whoever slaps you on your right cheek, turn the other to him also. If anyone wants to sue you and take away your tunic, let him have your cloak also. And whoever compels you to go one mile, go with him two (Matt. 5:38-41).

Are you someone who absolutely will not tolerate being walked all over? Do you fear that you will be known as a push-over? Of course, there are situations where you need to stand up for yourself. But do you *always* stand up for yourself? Can you stand no abuse towards your own person? Do you have suspicions about that man or that woman? Do you suspect they are out to take advantage of you? And what of it? The point is, wasting all of your energy trying to maintain your own reputation or to avoid all pitfalls in relationships or potential relationships shows a lack of Christian humility. Risk being taken advantage of for the glory of Christ.

Did we suddenly start thinking the church was about us, or that we needed to do the job of the Holy Spirit? Yes, there are other sides to this argument, other facets to church life. We need to watch out for wolves, and that is a job especially for pastors. But the text is making a certain point here. Paul is driving home the heart of the humility of Christian love. Open your heart and let the Word of God drive this truth into the center of your being. This is the heart of the Philippians mindset.

The Humility of Christ's Love

In fact, let us echo this call with Paul: "Let this mind be in you which was also in Christ Jesus." We have seen the Beauty of Christian love, the

Unity of Christian Love, the Humility of Christian Love, and now we see this Philippians mindset fleshed out in the Humility of Christ's love:

> Let this mind be in you which was also in Christ Jesus, who being in the form of God, did not consider it robbery to be equal with God, but made Himself of no reputation, taking the form of a bondservant, and coming in the likeness of men. And being found in appearance as a man, He humbled Himself and became obedient to the point of death, even the death of the cross (Phil. 2:5-8).

Just as water always finds the lowest place, so here we see the humility of the Son of God flow down, down, down to the very depths of death and Hell. This is the mindset we are to have as well. None of us can be the Messiah, but we are to reflect this downward flow of humility, this way of Christian love, that Jesus Christ displayed for all the world to see.

Already we should be completely overwhelmed. How can we go so low? How can we do as Jesus did? How can we love like Christ? There is no doubt about it, though- we are called to it: "Let this mind be in you". How can we achieve it? For those who are seasoned veterans in the fight of faith, they will be quick to admit that they fail over and over again to be humble and to clothe themselves in the love of Christ.

But it is in the very mindset of Jesus we see displayed here that we find our hope for living for Him in this way. Christ not only lived such a life to die as an example for us, he lived to die in order to give us the grace and the power and the Spirit by which we can die with Him and live with Him and reign with Him. It is in the truths surrounding the life and death and resurrection of Jesus Christ that we gain an understanding that we have been set free from the slavery of sin. Christians have been set free from slavery to selfish ambition and conceit. We have been set free from bondage to pride and self-serving, set free from the mindset of the world. We have been given the mind of Christ through faith in the gospel of Christ!

Here is the twin reality of the Christian life and of the Philippians mindset: We follow Christ because we trust in Him and we seek to live for Him only because He gives us the desire and the power to do so. We seek to grow in the grace and knowledge of Jesus Christ by taking up the means of grace. As we take up the means of grace God gives us grace to live for Him!

Let us put it this way, in the words of verses 12 and 13:

> Therefore, my beloved, as you have always obeyed, not as in my presence only, but now much more in my absence, work out your own salvation with fear and trembling; for it is God who works in you both to will and to do for His good pleasure.

Picture in your mind a man filling an immense hole with dirt. The hole needs to be filled in order for the man to be sanctified and be like Christ. The Gospel has given him a shovel and told him where the pile of dirt is which he can shovel into the hole. Every time the man shovels dirt in he finds that Christ is actually right there beside him shoveling in 10 times as much. And it is Christ through the gospel who keeps urging him to put in the shovel and to work at filling in the hole. But all the while, every time the man actually shovels in a shovel full of dirt, Christ has dumped in a loader's worth of soil.

We look like Christ the more we are reminded of and realize what He accomplished for us on the cross. You see, the story of Christ's humility in His life and death on the cross is not just a *pattern* for us, but this story is where we get the *power* to live the Christian life.

The heart of Christian living is centered in the Person who lived and died for sinners. We cannot travel far without gospel dependence upon the Lord Jesus Christ. For the Christian who tries to live without this dependence, may God have mercy and bring him quickly to a brokenness and fresh realization of his need for Christ and Him crucified.

The more we do for Christ and seek to be like Christ and seek to emulate the humility of Christian love, the more we must wash ourselves in the reality of the humility of Christ's love for His church. Here is where not only do we see a *pattern* and receive *power*, but we find *pardon* for our sins. "Pardon for sins of deepest dye". Pardon for the things you said you would never do when you came to Christ so many years ago. Pardon for pride, pardon for conceit, pardon for selfishness and self-seeking.

The Christian Life is surrounded behind, in front, and all around with Christ! "I have been crucified with Christ; it is no longer I who live, but Christ lives in me; and the life which I now live in the flesh I live by faith in the Son of God who loved me and gave himself for me" (Gal. 2:20).

A pattern for life, the power to live, and pardon for all our sins! O what a great salvation! Every spiritual blessing in the heavenly places in Christ![25] The hope of Glory: Christ in you![26]

As we go on year after year in the Christian life, we must adorn ourselves with the mind of Christ who served others to the bitter end. We must flow down like water to the lowest point, as Christ humbled Himself and became obedient to the point of death, even the death of the cross.

For those who seek the beauty of true Christian love in unity with those who are like-minded, in the humility that carries the mind of Christ- we will soon, very soon follow King Jesus in exaltation by His side. We will find our seat in the heavenly places in Christ, and we will follow the rest of mankind by bowing the knee to the King of glory. There we will know Jesus truly as Lord, and we will no longer fight or strive against His ways. No longer will our selfish ambition creep out from our hearts. No longer will we resist completely giving our all to the King. When the Kingdom of Heaven comes down to earth, the church will be in complete and sinless unity, wedded to the Head of the body, never to know division or schism of any kind ever again. And in that Eternal Day, the waters of peace and the fullness of God's Spirit will flow from the throne of the Father and the Lamb throughout the Bride

---

[25] Ephesians 1:3
[26] Colossians 1:27

of Christ with absolutely no hindrance or interruption. So, let us drink in of the heavenly realities as much as possible now in this battle ground of the current age. Let us usher in Christ's kingdom by renewing our minds in the likeness of our Savior.

Chapter Six

But what things were gain to me, these I have counted loss for Christ. Yet indeed I also count all things loss for the excellence of the knowledge of Christ Jesus my Lord, for whom I have suffered the loss of all things, and count them as rubbish, that I may gain Christ and be found in Him, not having my own righteousness, which is from the law, but that which is from God by faith; that I may know Him and the power of His resurrection, and the fellowship of His sufferings, being conformed to His death, if, by any means, I may attain to the resurrection from the dead. -Philippians 3:7-11

We have been looking at the texts in Philippians which contain the words "mind", "like-minded", or mental words such as "knowledge" and "know". The battle for the mind of the human soul is hot and raging, more than ever in this current age. Studying the Bible is a God-ordained means of driving into our hearts the word of God so that we may be transformed by the renewing of our minds.

But there is a problem. People today know so much, and yet they at the same time know so little. There is an absolute cram of knowledge being stuffed into the heads of men and women, boys and girls, at all hours of the day and night, it seems. Do we have room for a mindset that is saturated with God's word? Do we have room for the kind of knowledge the Bible tells us is worth more than gold or silver, worth more than life itself?

An article from *The Telegraph* by Richard Alleyne, science correspondent on February 11th, 2011 (now nearly a decade old) said the following:

> If you think that you are suffering from information overload then you may be right – a new study shows everyone is bom-

barded by the equivalent of 174 newspapers of data a day...
...The growth in the internet, 24-hour television and mobile
phones means that we now receive five times as much information every day as we did in 1986. But that pales into insignificance compared with the growth in the amount of information
we churn out through email, twitter, social networking sites
and text messages. Every day the average person produces six
newspapers worth of information compared with just two and
a half pages 24 years ago – nearly a 200-fold increase. All this
information needs storing and we now each have the equivalent of 600,000 books stored in computers, microchips and
even the strip on the back of your credit card. The extent of the
information revolution and digital age has been calculated by
Dr Martin Hilbert and his team at the University of southern
California."

How much of the 174 newspapers of data we ingest each day (notice I wrote "ingest" not "digest"- because people today seem to not have time to digest what they read and hear and see; they simply consume it and let it have its way with them for good or for ill)- brings health to our souls? How much of it is for the edification of our inner man? How much of it is counter-productive to spiritual growth? How much of it is simply vegetative-fill, or mindless entertainment? How much of it is actually *harmful* to the Christian life? When you or I analyze our daily data consumption in this way, what then is our prognosis for finishing the race well, for dying well, or for enduring hardships and persecutions?

Now, laying aside the data we must process in order to make a living, is the bulk of our consumption at this moment going to be worth much the day we stand before God? Paul says, "I count all things loss for the excellency of the knowledge of Christ Jesus my Lord". The word for knowledge here is the Greek word *gnoseos*. This is knowledge through experiential interaction. It is to know someone by experience. So, the question is do you *know* Jesus Christ? Not just know *about* Him? But knowing Him by experiencing a relationship with Him?

There is a ton of information out there, bombarding us daily: lots of events in the news each day, new laws being passed, new regulations in the workplace. What do we do with it all? What are we to do as Christians in this climate? …. COUNT ALL THINGS LOSS FOR THE EXCELLENCY OF THE KNOWLEDGE OF JESUS CHRIST!

We said in the last chapter that the heart of the Philippians mindset was Chapter 2:1-10. But this passage we are considering in this chapter is the heart of the heart of it all. This is the *one* thing we need to seek to do in life: grow in the grace and knowledge of Jesus Christ. If you are a Christian, the authority of God's word reveals to you that all your hope and comfort and wisdom and courage and strength and love and beauty and skill and piety is found in *knowing* Jesus. Not just professing faith in Him, but seeking to know Him, in experiential relationship.

In Him "are hidden all the treasures of wisdom and knowledge", we read in Colossians 2:3. Here in our text in Philippians we see that we are to seek to know Christ personally, in power, and in suffering. "That I may know Him and the power of His resurrection, and the fellowship of His sufferings, being conformed to His death, if by any means, I may attain to the resurrection from the dead."

To Know Christ Personally

Let us first explore some of the ways we can know Christ personally.

First of all, primarily, we know Him through His word. The Bible is not simply information about Christianity, nor a narrative of the history of Israel. The Scriptures are the very words of the Spirit of Christ. Through a meditation upon the parts and passages, through a concept of the whole counsel of God, through memorization, and through study- "Let the word of Christ dwell in you richly" (Col.3:16a).

"The word of God is living and active" (Heb. 4:12a). As you read it, and pray it into your heart, it has a way of working on you, long after you have closed the book itself and gone off to do your daily chores and labors. Many people have used the website Ancestry.com. It's a website where you can become a member and discover your family tree and your connections from hundreds of years ago. People can tie into other people's family trees and find information on their relatives from each other. One of the neat things about this website is that after you have found a few relatives on your tree, as it were, the website actually continues working while you are asleep. When you wake up the next day you will find several suggestions of connections the website has found through other archives and databases.

Well, the word of God is living and active and it works on us even when we are asleep, so to speak. The more we meditate on it, the more it will get into the recesses of our minds, and thus it will affect our words and actions. It can even affect our dreams. The course of God's commandments begins to work on us the moment we are saved. But the embers of the influence of His truth can burn low at different points in the Christian life. We need to continually stoke the fire, add logs to the flames, by seeking to grow in the knowledge of Christ through saturating ourselves in the word of God.

We need to mine the Scriptures. Often, the Bible will not yield to you its treasures without engaging in labor through study and prayerful meditation. To grow in the knowledge of Christ personally takes a drawing near on our part. But for every log we throw on the fire through seeking Christ in Scripture, the flames of the living and active word of God will grow bright and hot and yield light upon the path of our life.

Psalm 119:105-112:

> Your word is a lamp to my feet and a light to my path. I have sworn and confirmed that I will keep Your righteous judgments. I am afflicted very much; Revive me, O LORD, according to Your word. Accept, I pray, the freewill offering of my mouth, O LORD, and teach me your judgments. My life is continually in my hand, Yet I do not forget Your law. The wicked have laid a snare for me. Yet I have not strayed from

> your precepts. Your testimonies I have taken as a heritage forever, for they are the rejoicing of my heart. I have inclined my heart to perform Your statutes forever, to the very end.

Get the Bible into your blood stream and allow it to course through your mind and soul. Let the mind of Christ bring you into conformity to His image.

But then, we also know Christ personally through prayer. We listen to Him in His word, and we pray His word back to Him. We develop a habit, a default position of going to the throne of grace in prayer to seek mercy and to find grace to help during this difficult life. We run to Jesus in our prayers by casting our cares on Him, for He cares for us. We ask Him for wisdom in decisions we need to make; interceding for saints who need grace and guidance and more godliness; interceding for those who are lost and perishing without Christ; interceding for our enemies whom we are called to love. We speak to God through Christ by the Holy Spirit in praise, adoration, and exaltation of His excellency, His majesty, His goodness, His faithfulness, His love, His holiness, His justice, His mercy, His grace, His benevolence, His Providence, His Sovereignty, His Omnipotent Power, His Omniscient Knowledge, His Beauty, His Glory, His Decree, His Salvation, His Fatherhood, His Guidance, His care for our souls and His Artistic Wonder as Creator.

We pray to Him in thanksgiving for all His provisions, and all His special mercies. We intercede for rulers and all who are in authority that we may live a quiet and peaceable life. We intercede in prayer for the church across the world, for our brothers and sisters and their children who are being persecuted. We pray for the economy and for prosperity in order to gather resources for the furtherance of the kingdom of God and the strengthening of families and societies in stability and order. We also pray for the punishment of evil doers.

In all this we grow to know Christ personally as we spend time in prayer to Him, through Him, for Him.

We also grow in the knowledge of Christ personally by worshiping Him. All of life should be worship, but we are writing here of those special times of worship as we sing hymns and spiritual songs and make music to the glory of His name. As we sing praise to Him and pray to Him through song and music, we consider the words we are singing and make effort to bring our thoughts in line with the words and to take our thoughts captive to the obedience of Christ. We engage in making a sacrifice of joy when we might be feeling dull or depressed. We praise the living God in songs of joy. We glorify the living God in songs of minor key that reflect in soberness upon the cross and upon sin and upon suffering for His name. A major part of growing in the knowledge of Christ is how we are conformed into His likeness as we sing spiritual songs and hymns to glorify Him and to adore Him and to love Him.

We also grow in knowledge of His person through the fellowship of the Son of God. This is what permeates all we have been discussing: fellowship with Christ. Knowing Him in relationship. Thinking upon Him as friend and elder brother. Resting in Him as savior, shepherd, and king. Looking for Him. Longing for Him. Delighting in Him. Devoting your life to bringing others into this fellowship of the Son of God. When you speak, it is as speaking the oracles of God. When you use your hands, it is as being the healing hands of Jesus. When you walk, it is with feet shod for the preparation of the gospel of peace (Eph. 6:15). All to know Jesus and to make Him known!

To Know Christ in Power

But secondly, we know Him in power, in the power of His resurrection. In fact, you cannot know Christ personally, unless you have known Him in power. Again, known Him in the power of His resurrection. When Jesus Christ died on the cross to take upon Himself the wrath of God against sins, because He was the Son of God, divine yet also fully human-death could not hold Him down. The wages of sin is death, but Christ Himself had no sin. He was made sin on the cross and all of God's wrath and hate and anger against sin was poured out upon Him as if He were responsible for all the sins of the elect. But because He Himself was sinless, death could not keep its grip on Him. He rose from the dead! And because Christ rose, He brings life to all those for whom He died for!

People once dead in sin, people once blind to the truth, people once foolish and ignorant as to the existence of God and their nature as children of His wrath- now, Christ gives these people spiritual life! The Spirit of Christ regenerates the spiritually dead person, gives them faith to believe Christ died for them, and justifies them from the law of God they had broken.

This is all possible because of the life of Christ and because He rose from the dead. Christ gives us newness of life. It is the power of His resurrection. This also sets us free from the tyranny of sin. We are no longer slaves to sin because of the resurrection power of Jesus. Romans 6:5-14,

> For if we have been united together in the likeness of His death, certainly we also shall be in the likeness of His resurrection, knowing this, that our old man was crucified with Him, that the body of sin might be done away with, that we should no longer be slaves of sin. For he who has died has been freed from sin. Now if we died with Christ, we believe that we shall also live with Him, knowing that Christ, having been raised from the dead, dies no more. Death no longer has dominion over Him. For the death that He died, He died to sin once for all, but the life that He lives, He lives to God. Likewise you also, reckon yourselves to be dead indeed to sin, but alive to God in Christ Jesus our Lord. Therefore do not let sin reign in your mortal body, that you should obey its lusts. And do not present your members as instruments of unrighteousness to sin, but present yourselves to God as being alive from the dead, and your members as instruments of righteousness to God. For sin shall not have dominion over you, for you are not under law but under grace.

You see, because of the resurrection power of Christ, Christians now have the ability to choose not to sin. They have the ability to resist the devil. They have the ability to live to the glory of God! Those who do not know Christ are unable to do this. They have not known the power of His resurrection. They do not yet know the liberty of having their natures led out of death to the heavenly places in Christ. He is the Captain of salvation who rose from the dead and sat down at the right hand of God, having defeated sin, death, and the Devil.

Do you just know about Jesus? Or do you *know* Christ? Do you know him according to the power of His resurrection? Are you a Christian burdened down by habitual sins? Is your conscience suffering because you have been sliding backwards? This text above in Romans 6 is for you to meditate upon. What does it all mean? Is it true? Why are you struggling? What is the way out? Have you known the power of His resurrection? What does it take to tap back into that knowledge? None of these words you are reading might dislodge you from your present position of backsliding or discouragement, but allow them to point out to you the mines where riches untold can be found that will set you free from your seemingly spiritual poverty.

How badly do you desire to grow in the knowledge of Christ? How long will you study the Scriptures until you find a promise becomes alive and meaningful to you? How long will you meditate upon what Christ has done for you until you find the power is broken of some habitual sin you have been nursing? 2 Peter 1:2-4 says,

> Grace and peace be multiplied to you in the knowledge of God and of Jesus our Lord, as His divine power has given to us all things that pertain to life and godliness, through the knowledge of Him who called us by glory and virtue, by which have been given to us exceedingly great and precious promises, that through these you may be partakers of the divine nature, having escaped the corruption that is in the world through lust.

To know Christ in Suffering

One of the implicit promises in the New Testament is that if you have been born again you know resurrection power. We are to know Christ in person and in power. But thirdly, we know Him in suffering. Again, our text: "That I may know Him and the power of His resurrection, and the fellowship of His sufferings, being conformed to His death, if, by any means, I may attain to the resurrection from the dead."

If you are a Christian following Jesus, you no doubt have known or will very soon come to know *suffering*. We grow to know Christ Jesus through our experiences of suffering during these travelling days of the Christian life. Our knowledge of Christ through suffering happens in several ways.

First of all, we know Christ through suffering in our struggle against sin- against ourselves, really. Some believers wish that this was not the case- that they could get to a place where they have arrived in the Christian life. We will see in our next chapter that no one has arrived in the Christian life during this present lifetime. But when a believer is young or immature, he often becomes confused about the tensions in the Christian life. Why is it just when it seems as if I can finally be who I want to be in Christ- being the man or woman who emulates stability and godliness at all times, who is always patient in trying circumstances, who only loves when ridiculed, who never feels tempted to do things that he thinks no Christian would ever do, who is always filled with a zeal and a hunger for God and His word- why is it just when I think I might have come over the ridge into green pastures, that my spiritual "car" breaks down again or blows a tire?

As we mature in Christ, we begin to embrace the tension between still knowing sin within us (with all the pain and embarrassment that brings), and growing more and more accustomed to running to Christ and rehearsing the gospel in our minds and hearts. We become familiar with washing ourselves in the truths of our justification and embracing the humility of being a broken and contrite sinner before the presence of God.

The mature Christian begins to know the rhythm of knowing sweet fellowship with the Son of God but then also knowing the sweet pain of conviction of sin. Maturity in Christ sees us growing in the freeing grace of repentance and feeding upon the milk of the gospel again and again. And whereas oftentimes the young believer is confused by this tension and this ebb and flow, the mature believer has embraced what we could really call *suffering* in our fight against sin.

We Know Christ by fellowshipping in His sufferings in this way. Now Christ Himself did not suffer in sinning Himself, but He did endure temptations. He was tempted in every point we will be, yet without sin. He was exposed to the ravages and the effects of sin all around Him as He lived and walked on this earth. Just as Christ knew the tension of being the Son of God in all His holiness and glory and sinlessness versus being made human flesh and living amongst all the filth of sin in this world, while also being tempted full force by the devil all throughout His life on earth- so too we fellowship in His sufferings through our fight against sin in the tensions of the Christian life of being new creatures in Christ Jesus, yet still having the carcass of indwelling sin to drag around with us wherever we go.

We grow in our knowledge of Christ through fellowshipping with Him in His sufferings through our growing hatred of sin as we suffer its pull upon our hearts. At the same time, we grow in our desire and hunger for holiness and the presence of God in our lives. Christ suffered not only by His death on the cross, but by His life. The very fact that He was made incarnate and His Godhead was veiled, and that in His humanity He was not yet seated at the right hand of God; the very fact that while on this earth He looked to Jerusalem knowing His task to suffer the wrath of God against sin remained unfinished- this was a form of suffering for the God-man.

Likewise, as we run the race of the Christian life, we suffer in knowing we must continue for the time being in these sinful bodies and wait patiently for sinless glory in the presence of the King. In other words, pining for glory is a form of suffering! We might not be able to compare it with the suffering of the persecuted or of those afflicted with severe trials, but the closer we grow to Christ the more this fight against sin and this waiting for glory is a kind of suffering.

But we also fellowship in the sufferings of Christ in our growing estrangement from the world and our loss of appetite for its dainties. The principles of Babylon (this world system of the evil age) rub us the wrong way as we grow into Christ's likeness. We begin to realize more and more that we are not citizens of this world, but citizens of heaven. The trinkets and pleasures of Vanity Fair have no draw upon our souls, and we begin to stand out for our "narrowmindedness" and "intolerance".

This all, of course, eventually draws us into receiving persecution from a world that hates the light it sees reflected from us. No doubt, Jesus Christ suffered in this way. Though His Godhead was veiled, His spiritual light as the Son of God nevertheless penetrated all who heard Him speak, heard of His deeds, or saw Him. As His pure, holy light of truth and goodness shone into the darkened hearts of the people of this world, they hated Him for exposing their wicked hearts to themselves and to others around them.

This is why the world hates Christians. We remind them of their sin. We remind them of the judgment to come. We remind them of their hypocrisy and cowardliness. Who can stand a dripping faucet when they are trying to sleep? We will do whatever it takes to silence the annoying sound. This is what persecution is, to put it mildly. The world trying to shut up the dripping faucet of the voice of Christ in His church.

And so, we know Christ through fellowshipping with Him in this kind of suffering. The world's hatred and animosity towards us makes eternal matters clearer to us. We see the value of the things of God more distinctly. The things of this world grow strangely dim.

This persecution also comes in the form of spiritual warfare. As we shine more and more brightly for the cause of the kingdom of God, the spiritual forces of wickedness will take notice of us and they will take action to silence our witness. They will stir up persecution, conjure up temptations, and try to destroy us through orchestrating various dangers to our body and soul.

To fellowship in Christ's sufferings in these ways is to be conformed to His death. We cannot be children of God without being conformed to the death of Christ in these ways. O'Brien notes that these are "the birth pangs of the Messiah, which fall upon God's people. All Christians participate in these sufferings; through them they enter the kingdom of God."[27]

Paul writes in 2 Corinthians 4:7-9,

> But we have this treasure in earthen vessels, that the excellence of the power may be of God and not of us. We are hard pressed on every side, yet not crushed; we are perplexed, but not in despair; persecuted, but not forsaken; struck down, but not destroyed- always carrying about in the body the dying of the Lord Jesus, that the life of Jesus also may be manifested in our body...

He says in 1:5, "For as the sufferings of Christ abound in us, so our consolation also abound through Christ." He writes in 6:10 that as ministers of God they are "as sorrowful, yet always rejoicing; as poor, yet making many rich; as having nothing, and yet possessing all things." Jesus was not a rich man. Christ had nowhere to lay His head. Poverty is not a sign of being faithless. As a Christian, it can many times be a way of fellowshipping in the sufferings of Christ.

What about illness or disease that we have not experienced because of serving the gospel of Jesus Christ? What if I am ill because of previous sin before I was a Christian? What if I have cancer just because of genetics? Is that fellowshipping in the sufferings of Christ?

We would argue that ALL hardships in this world are ultimately a result of sin. Maybe a hardship is not because of sin you directly committed, but because this is a sin-cursed world, death and suffering and

---

[27] Peter O'Brien. *The Epistle to the Philippians, The New International Greek Testament Commentary* (Wm. B. Eerdmans Publishing Co., 1991), 406

toil and hardship has entered the scene. Spending time as a believer in the hospital as your body suffers from disease or affliction not caused when engaged in a direct "ministry" of the gospel, is indeed a suffering that can draw us deeper into the knowledge of Christ.

As a Christian, when you battle these things you are battling them as a citizen of heaven. As your body aches, you long for the day of a glorified body. As you come in and out of consciousness and see your loved ones visiting you, your heart sees and longs for eternity clearer, and you see that you are a debtor to all men to point them to the Lord Jesus Christ.

We would also argue that all suffering in the Christian life is used by God to bring us into a deeper knowledge of Christ. As you struggle to make ends meet, or to learn the new job that is overwhelming you, you do so as one who knows all hardships are because this world is destined to perish by fire. So we would argue that as the waters of the curse of sin wash over you in this life, you are indeed growing in the knowledge of Christ as He uses it all to cause you to pine more and more for heaven and glory and to hate what sin has done to this world and to humanity.

Did not Jesus weep at the tomb of Lazarus? Was He not weeping because of what sin has done to this world? Was it not due to the death and confusion sin has brought? Was Jesus not suffering while on this earth in such a way? So too, the Christian is fellowshipping in Christ's sufferings through life's difficulties and hardships knowing it is the result of Adam's sin and our participation in his likeness.

We must know Christ personally, in power, and in His sufferings if by any means we will attain to the resurrection from the dead. Are you not familiar with Christ in these ways? Do you *know* Him? You can know all of the current trends in theological debates, you can know all the answers to the catechism, but do you *know* the fellowship of the Son of God? The *one* thing we must seek to do in life is to know Jesus Christ. Count all things loss in relation to this! What is distracting you from this one goal? Did you begin the race of the Christian life well? Are you going to finish well? Hebrews 12:1,2 exhorts us:

> Therefore we also, since we are surrounded by so great a cloud of witnesses, let us lay aside every weight, and the sin which so easily ensnares us, and let us run with endurance the race that is set before us, looking unto Jesus, the author and finisher of our faith, who for the joy that was set before Him endured the cross, despising the shame, and has sat down at the right hand of the throne of God.

In verse 11 of Philippians 3 Paul says, "if by any means I may attain to the resurrection of the dead" It would be better translated "if I may *reach* the resurrection of the dead"[28]. Here Paul is speaking of that final resurrection when the saints are glorified. Through knowing Jesus, we will find ourselves arriving at the final resurrection one day.

Count all things loss for the excellency of the knowledge of Jesus Christ your Savior. Now, if all of this seems totally strange to you and if you are not moved to desire to know Jesus Christ with your life's aim- then, dear reader, you are standing over Hell on a thin sheet of ice. You cannot be a true Christian and not desire to know Christ in these ways. However, the good news is the door is open to you to come in and cast yourself on the mercy of Christ and ask Him to make your life about Him and for Him and to reflect Him and to save you from yourself. Cry out to Him to save you from the sins that entangle you again and again, enslaving you deeper and deeper as the years pass and the emptiness remains. Sinner- come to Jesus Christ and buy gold refined in the fire. Come to Jesus through faith alone and receive forgiveness and a spiritual nature that desires God. Come begin an eternity of growing in the knowledge of the God who made you and who holds the universe in His hands, He who has arranged all the universe so that you would be reading this right at this moment.

---

[28] Ibid., 382

Chapter Seven

Not that I have already attained, or am already perfected; but I press on, that I may lay hold of that for which Christ has also laid hold of me. Brethren, I do not count myself to have apprehended; but one thing I do, forgetting those things which are behind and reaching forward to those things which are ahead, I press toward the goal for the prize of the upward call of God in Christ Jesus. Therefore let us, as many as are mature, have this mind; and if in anything you think otherwise, God will reveal even this to you. Nevertheless, to the degree that we have already attained, let us walk by the same rule, let us be of the same mind. –Philippians 3:13-16

What would it be like for you to make it to the top of your idea of success? No doubt we all have or have had dreams and fantasies of that perfect job, that perfect income bracket, that perfect lottery ticket number, that perfect neighborhood with the perfect house. We have all probably had the tendency at some point in our lives to longingly imagine ourselves in some position, some place, having some kind of vision for our lives.

Children do it too. Do you remember fantasizing as a young child of what you wanted to do when you grew up? Some children might think Ryan, of the Youtube.com channel *Ryan's World* has made it to the top of his wildest dreams. Listen to some of this article from *Business Insider*:

> 8-year-old Ryan Kaji of YouTube's Ryan's World (formerly Ryan Toys Review) is the highest-paid YouTube star in the world, and has built a business empire from reviewing toys — with help from his parents. Kaji earned an estimated $26 million, according to Forbes, based on pretax figures from June

2018 to June 2019. That's a jump from the $22 million Kaji earned the previous year.[29]

In case you didn't know, Ryan's World is a youtube.com channel where little Ryan basically opens and plays with the latest new toys on the market, and parents love how it keeps their little ones engrossed and quietly watching.

26 million dollars in one year! That's a lot of responsibility to be beginning life with. What would you do if you started life with over 26 million dollars (and that's just one year's worth of income for Ryan)? The point we want to make in this is that the news and the internet thrive on stories like this. People love hearing about other people (kids!) who suddenly land on an incredible fortune.

This world system is fueled by motivating its members into striving to get to the place of their dreams. It feeds the cravings and the desires to get to that place of seemingly total ease, fun, wealth, and beauty. The world constantly tells us that we need to get to the top, we need to make it big, we need to achieve the good life, and that we need to escape the drudgery of the common horde.

These principles we bring with us into the Christian life. Often, we view our relationship with Christ and His gospel as something that will see us get to a place where what life and the Devil try to throw at us will just bounce off. We seek to get to the spiritual good life. We imagine getting to a certain plateau of special spiritual existence in this life. We seek to get to a place where we might have a stoic kind of resistance to anything that might precipitate unwanted emotions, fears, anxieties, disappointments, or desires. What we really sometimes imagine, in other words, is that we can *arrive* in the Christian life.

Now, in our text Paul specifically says "Not that I have already attained, or am already perfected….brethren I do not count myself to have apprehended." We see in this text that we cannot expect to arrive or to apprehend or to reach perfection in this current life. But does that mean

---

[29] https://www.businessinsider.com/ryans-world-boy-makes-26-million-per-year-on-youtube-2019-12

we should completely jettison all of our dreams and desires to get to some "place" that we aren't at right now? Are we to not have any dreams at all? Are we not to seek to get to a more mature place in the Christian life than we are at right now?

We see also in this passage that Paul says, "But I press on…one thing I do….reaching forward to those things which are ahead, I press toward the goal of the upward call of God in Christ Jesus." What we are seeing in this section of Philippians is the tension between realizing we have not arrived and seeking, *pressing* forward towards a goal of full maturity in Christ Jesus. Paul says in verse 15, "Therefore let us, as many as are mature, have this mind." The Philippians mindset of a mature Christian is embracing the fact that we have not arrived, and yet that we are to continually press forward to gain a full hold on Christ and His likeness.

Verse 12 is really the core of the idea in this passage before us: "Not that I have already attained, or am already perfected; but I press on, that I may lay hold of that for which Christ Jesus has also laid hold of me." Verses 13 and 14 are really just an amplification of verse 12, a more detailed explosion of what Paul has already said in verse 12. He's saying the same thing as in verse 12, just further articulated: "Brethren, I do not count myself to have apprehended; but one thing I do , forgetting those things which are behind and reaching forward to those things which are ahead, I press toward the goal for the prize of the upward call of God in Christ Jesus." Understanding this mindset and embracing it is the way to maturity in Christ.

As we consider this passage we will first look at considering ourselves as always wanting; next we will think about not considering anything about ourselves; and finally we will ponder only considering one thing in life.

Considering Ourselves as Always Wanting

Another way to phrase the above heading is, we have not arrived. Really, it should be phrased that we will never arrive, at least on this side of eternity. Now, is not that depressing? Is it not a horrible outlook on life to think that you will never get to a place of fullness, of wholeness, a place of true maturity? How can we be motivated to do anything, to pursue any kind of good work, to look to grow in Christ if we are to consider ourselves as always wanting, never attaining, never arriving?

Let us think of this confession of Paul (that he says he had not arrived) in the context of the rest of the book of Philippians and the rest of Paul's epistles. Paul is continually revealing truth to the churches as an apostle in all his letters to the churches. He is exhorting, he is rebuking, he is encouraging. He does it all with the underlying idea that we are to imitate him as he imitated Christ.

Paul was no doubt admired by many who loved the Lord Jesus Christ in the early church. He filled up in his flesh what was lacking in the afflictions of Christ for the sake of the church. He suffered over and over again to bring the gospel to the world, and to shepherd the souls of the saints in the churches he had planted. Paul's daily concern was for the churches. Many in the early church were no doubt aware of Paul's deep love and concern for them.

Think of what we read here in the book of Philippians. In 1:3: "I thank my God upon every remembrance of you, always in every prayer of mine with joy for your fellowship in the gospel from the first day until now." In 1 Thessalonians 2:7,8 he writes, "But we were gentle among you, just as a nursing mother cherishes her own children. So, affectionately longing for you, we were well pleased to impart to you not only the gospel of God, but also our very own lives, because you had become dear to us." Throughout Paul's writings he calls the church his beloved and his brethren. These were not just cliché, throw away words for Paul!

Paul's reputation continues to this day in the church of Jesus Christ. It is a reputation of maturity and selflessness, of love and godliness. Paul fills his epistles with theological encouragements and imperatives for the church to live by, and through it all he calls them to follow his example.

Perhaps you have known someone like this in your life. They seem to have it all together. Nothing seems to shake them or dislodge them from a position of being the ultimate role-model. And at some point, they try to encourage you in your walk with the Lord or in your difficult situation. Do not we often think when these kinds of people offer us council or advice: "Well, it's easy for you to talk about how to deal with this! You never struggle with sin like I do, you do not have these difficulties I have."

We can imagine that maybe some in the early church might have felt that same way about Paul. They thought: "Paul, you can tell me what Christ did for me and how I can live for Him, but it's easy for you! You have had supernatural visitations from Christ! You have actually seen Him! You have been called by God to be an apostle!"

Paul seems to answer this kind of issue some might be having with him by saying, "Not that I have already attained, or am already perfected." He just got done a few verses before saying he counted all things loss for the excellency of the knowledge of Jesus Christ. We think, "Wow! Who really lives like that? Paul, you are way beyond me. Can you even relate to me?"

Paul gives an insight into his mindset to the Philippians by saying that he considers himself as always wanting (Of course, David says in Psalm 23 "I shall not want", but we are writing here about a want in regards to full maturity, not in regards to having our needs taken care of by God). He never considers himself to have attained. He says, "Not that I have already attained."

Paul did not sit down at night and camp out on thoughts about himself, about how godly he was, or to what an amazing degree of spirituality he had attained. Paul does not seem to be the type of guy that assessed the accomplishments in his own character growth very much; not to the degree that many of us may often do. He did not admire himself and his great growth in the Lord the way 21st century believers may sometimes do.

Furthermore, Paul did not say this: that he had not attained, as some kind of nod to humility on his part. It was not to meet his quota of godly sayings for the day. This was a mindset Paul was fully given over to. His right hand of need for growth in Christ never knew what his left hand of depth of godliness was doing, to put it another way.

No, Paul no doubt understood that he had been given great grace. He knew he was an apostle and he knew he was a leader in the church. He did not have some kind of false humility that put himself down to the degree that he could not stand up and lead others. He poured out the wisdom he had been given to the church whenever he could.

But that is just it: He understood that all of these things about him were the grace of God. They were gifts that had been given to him for the sake of the church and the glory of Christ. Paul knew he was merely a steward of the apostleship, he was a steward of the gospel, he was a steward of the love of God in Christ Jesus. All of these things in Him were given for the glory of God. When Paul did meet with God in prayer and worship and fellowship, he did not do so bringing to God all of his so-called accomplishments as something he could bring as collateral to impress God with and to earn His favor. As he stood before the mirror of God's word in deeper and deeper labor and study and in seeking Christ and in preaching Christ- he truly, purely, honestly realized that he was in desperate need of the mercy of God! He saw himself truly, purely, honestly as the chief of sinners.

Think of it! He was aware of so much grace in his life. He had seen the risen Christ on the road to Damascus. He had received direct revelation from the Spirit of God. He knew so much and he had experienced so much. Yet in the face of it all, in the light of all the grace, Paul continued to fail each day like all Christians do. He made mistakes. He sinned against God by his actions, thoughts, words, motives. And this was done in the face of all the revelation he had received! Therefore, the more Paul knew, the more he considered himself as wanting. He knew deeply that he was not perfected.

Now, we can relate to Paul. How many Bibles do we have in our homes? What kind of access do we have to Christian literature? What kind of access do we have to good preaching? How much teaching have we received in good, sound theology? With all of the tools and riches we have as an American church, what simple, little things can distract us from seeking to know Christ? What light pressures can make us snap in sinful anger, or sinful anxieties? How elusive can our pride be, so much so that maybe there are some reading this who think they do not struggle with pride?

O, we know we have not attained! Now, how is this an encouragement to us? Because Paul was in the same boat as you, dear Christian! Paul was not supernatural. He was natural, and that included struggling with the same kinds of things we all struggle with. We are always going to be wanting, needing to grow in the knowledge of Christ! It is not to excuse our sin, or to cause us to feel fine with coasting and drifting. But it is to encourage us that the Holy Spirit knows and understands our lives! He wants you to know He knows right where you are!

He knows you are not going to arrive in this life! "There is therefore now no condemnation for those who are in Christ Jesus!"(Rom 8:1a) The Spirit used Paul as a leader and as an example, but Paul didn't teach from house to house in a detached manner! No doubt he learned through many failures to get to the level of maturity he had achieved in Christ. And he surely consoled those in the early church by sharing the struggles God had brought him through. When a brother in Philippi shared with him his struggle with fear, Paul could say "I have often had fears within" or, "I've despaired of life at times".

The Spirit of God places Paul as a primary writer of the New Testament so that we can not only imitate him but also so that we can relate to him! It seems like in the 21st century the church misses out many times on the fact that the New Testament epistles were written partially by men whom we are supposed to relate to and find encouragement from their lives. Because their lives were similar to ours in many ways!

Do you consider yourself often as wanting in different areas? You are supposed to! Do you feel like you fall so short of being Christ like? You are supposed to! Or does your pride tell you that you should be feeling different at some point? Do you imagine yourself getting to that level where you can camp out on thinking about your godliness and your depth of character? Do you *really* want to be like that? That is actually sick. But guess what, we have all done that at some point or another.

That is the point! Realize that about yourself! We all have planks in our eyes. None of us pray like we should. None of us do *all* to the glory of God. None of us meditate on the word of God like we should. Again, the point is not to excuse our failures! It is for us to rest in the fact that God has ordained our sanctification in Christ and we are right where He knew we would be right now and that if we are in Christ he *will* complete what He started in us!

Still, Paul had been used in amazing ways for the Lord. He knew this. If you are a Christian, you know you have been used by God at times. Some reading this may have been used in amazing ways. Maybe you have led someone to Christ, or maybe you have given some of your finances to the cause of the kingdom so that you had to make real sacrifices. Sometimes we display real holiness that brings great glory to God. Without holiness no one will see the Lord, the Bible says. If you are born again, you *have* displayed holiness at times. You cannot be a Christian and not have some holiness.

What do we do with all of this? With memories of amazing times in the service of God, and with regrets of great failures in the Lord at the same time? What do we do with getting to wonderful plateaus in the Christian life where we feel we have come so far, and then with times of sliding backwards and regressing and returning to former sins?

Forget it all. Yes, forget it. It is not that we act stupid and naïve and do not know about our own lives, about what we have done or have not done. But we are to, in a way, not consider anything about ourselves.

Not Considering Anything about Ourselves

Verse 13, "Brethren, I do not count myself to have apprehended: but one thing I do, forgetting those things which are behind…." This is the key to staying focused on Christ, focused on the finish line, and to being able to continue on despite life's regrets. It is the key to moving on despite the scars that remind us of painful memories, despite the constant failures in so many areas, despite being a Christian for 20, 30, 40 years and being so stunted from who you know you should be in Christ.

Forget the things that are behind you. Release your grip of bitterness, of pain, of regret and let the past fall under the blood of Jesus. Rise from the ashes afresh and anew in clean linens, in the righteousness of Christ, and start moving forward again, step by step.

You cannot fix those things you regret so much. You are not able to redo those times in your life. You cannot help yourself by fretting over the things that are behind over and over again in your mind, wishing things had turned out different, wishing those things never happened, staring in amazement at your life in such a way that you cannot believe those things ever happened. You say, "I cannot believe life is really happening to me this way. I cannot believe life has taken the turn it has for me." No…forget.

The Greek word here for forgetting, *epilanthanomenos*, is a present middle participle, which means it is describing an action Paul is continually doing. This is Paul's continuous effort: to allow the memories of pain and regret to continually be shed from his meditations. It is not something you just do at different stages in your life. It is a continuous action for the Christian.

When we hold on to the past, we cannot move forward. To move forward is life. It is where we need to go. But it is not just the difficult memories of the past we are to continuously forget. In order to move forward we must not get bogged down in pride, narcissistic tendencies, or in gloating over our accomplishments. We are to forget *continuously* things that God has accomplished through us and things that God has accomplished in us.

Of course, we are to thank him for amazing grace. We are not naïve as to where we have come from and how far we have traveled. It is instead that we are not to settle down and preen ourselves and look in the spiritual mirror in order to gape in admiration at ourselves. We should avoid thinking and replaying over and over again something we accomplished, all the while admiring how well we handled ourselves.

We are to continuously forget the laurels that have been awarded us in this life. Again, it can be difficult to try to describe what Paul is saying here due to semantics. Paul is not saying you cannot enjoy what God has accomplished in you and through you. But we must be careful to quickly forget the *me* part of it all. We must grow in amazement at what *God* has done and give Him the glory and the credit. To continuously forget in this way keeps us honestly humble before the Lord.

You might say, "Well, how can I ever take pride in something I have done?" It is one thing to end the day's work and to be thankful and admire what God did through you; to be pleased with what you have accomplished that day. It is one thing to drive by something you have helped build and to think, "Wow, we did a good job on that!" But it is quite another thing to look at some element of labor or work you have accomplished every day and to think, "What a good job *I* did! What a good boy am I!" Every day we can be stroking our pride for how hard we work, how precise we are, how holy we are, how nice we are, how helpful we are, how neat we are, how good looking we are, how smart we are, how much we read, how good we are at playing an instrument or at being able to make art, or being able to speak another language, or at having preached a sermon, or having performed a medical procedure, or having saved someone's life, or having given someone financial help. Whatever it is, whatever is now behind us, we are to continuously forget.

This Greek word for forgetting means actually: to overlook. Stop looking at yourself in the mirror, as it were. Forget what you look like. We are not to consider anything about ourselves. This is not about you. This is all about God and His glory. Anything you have done is merely a gift, a stewardship given to you by God. Admiring ourselves, considering ourselves in such a way that we gaze starry-eyed at our success or our accomplishments is really a ridiculous thing in light of the fact that we are created beings who have nothing apart from the graces and gifts of God.

So, overlook in yourself what someone might think is amazing in you. Overlook the fact that you have moved up in position at work or in school. Overlook how amazing your craftsmanship turns out- so that you can reach forward to grab hold of the likeness of Jesus Christ. You see, we can't move forward, we can't reach forward to Christ and His likeness, if we are bogged down with stroking our pride and our ego and replaying in our minds over and over again everything we think we have done well.

Only Considering One Thing in Life

"But one thing I do, forgetting those things which are behind and reaching forward to those things which are ahead. I press toward the goal for the prize of the upward call of God in Christ Jesus." The Greek word for reaching forward is also a present middle participle, so it is this continuous action. It means to stretch out, to strain. Paul viewed his life as a Christian as continually straining forward, stretching out with all his fibers to reach the finish line.

You see, we are really only to consider one thing in life. We are to press towards the goal. We are to stretch out to reach the finish line with all that is within us, with all our resources, with all our mental faculties, with all the love we have, with all the gifts we have, with all the power and intelligence we can muster.

When I ran cross country and track in high school, one of the things our coach told us to never ever do during a race was to look back over your shoulder to see who was behind you. You never ever do that! Even when you sense someone is bearing down on you, you keep your head facing forward, you look towards the prize, towards the goal. You bear down on the finish line with every muscle in your body. That is how you win races. That is how you finish well. When you get your mind on the guy next to you or the guy behind you, or the people in the crowd- you lose focus and start slowing down unconsciously. You lose your resolve to get to the finish line. You should not care about the other runners- your goal is the tape. Your one desire is to get across the finish line.

That is exactly what the Greek is portraying here in verse 14. The one thing we are to consider in life is reaching the goal of finishing our course by bringing maximum glory to God while looking as much according to the image of Christ as we can by the grace of God. It is to walk with as much holiness as we can into the works God has prepared beforehand for us to walk in. It is to strive with all we are, with all we have, to live for the cause of the kingdom and to break the tape at the end of our lives in order to enter into the presence of the Master and hear Him say, "Well done!"

The upward call of Christ Jesus, according to some commentators, reflects a practice in Greek games and contests where the victor received an 'upward call' to step up before the king or the emperor and receive their prize. O'Brien notes,

> In the Panhellenic games (Like those at Olympia), which were organized and presided over by highly respected officers called Hellendodikai, the successful athlete was summoned to receive his prize from their hands. F.F. Bruce, with reference to a similar Roman practice has claimed: 'On special occasion in Rome this call might come from the Emperor himself; how proudly the successful athlete would obey the summons and step up to the imperial box to accept the award.[30]

This pales so much in comparison to the upward call of God in Christ Jesus. Saints will be summoned before the throne to receive an imperishable crown and be told from the King Himself, "Well done, good and faithful servant." This is the one thing we should be considering in life. All of our decisions and considerations, all of our purchases and desires for spending, all of our life should be considering the one goal, the one prize: the upward call of God in Christ Jesus. Let this thought move

---

[30] Peter O'Brien. *The Epistle to the Philippians, The New International Greek Testament Commentary* (Wm. B. Eerdmans Publishing Co., 1991), 431-432

you, Christian! Stir yourself to live to the glory of God with the thought of the upward call!

Indeed, this will be the moment all of your life was meant to lead up to. It will be the moment you are decorated for service and battle in the name of King Jesus. You will adorn your heavenly uniform, as it were, which you will wear for all eternity and which will shine forth forever the capacity of glory according to the life God gave you the grace to live.

I have known Christians who have basically determined within themselves to just get by. They were happy to just "squeak" into heaven. They understand enough of soteriology (the doctrine of salvation) to trust that they are saved. But they have not thought to really strive for the kingdom of God. They make little effort to think of doing all they can to win the prize. Their lives consist of enjoying hobbies and recreation and being with friends and family almost as an end in themselves. Of course, these are good things God gives us to enjoy, but the kinds of Christians we are considering are only really concerned with these peripheral gifts God has given them. They have no desire to do all they can to finish well. They are not concerning themselves with holiness or with avoiding love for the world and the things of the world. They do not put effort into growing in the grace and knowledge of Christ Jesus apart from showing up each Lord's Day to hear the sermon and then go home and put their Bible back on the shelf until the next Sunday.

There will be a day when saints will receive the upward call. I can guarantee that when you are standing in glory at that time, you will wish with everything in you that you had pressed with all your might while you were on this earth to glorify Jesus. You will see believers receiving praise and commendation from the King of the Universe! You will see the last finally become first and be decked out by Jesus Himself with robes of glory that He specially prepared for them to wear for all eternity. Robes shining in His righteousness (yes, you cannot be a saint and not have that) but also robes somehow reflecting the things they did in this life; the thoughts they thought, the love by which they loved, the gifts they gave from, the deaths they died- all by the grace of God and for the glory of God.

Of course, all of it will be a gift of God. Of course, God will get all the glory. Yes, you are His workmanship created in Christ Jesus for good works. We cannot pull motivation to strive and to stretch forward for the glory of God unless we have known the saving power of Christ Jesus in regard to our sins. We cannot be stirred to have the Philippians mindset unless Christ Jesus has laid hold of us in the first place. None of us has apprehended, none of us has attained.

But does this mindset resonate with your soul? Do you long to live for Jesus- to press towards the mark? This is only possible because you have cast yourself upon Him for salvation. If you long for this mindset to be yours, if you long to have this kind of mature tension: embracing the reality that you are always going to be wanting and never considering yourself, and yet continuously pressing forward; if the truth of this passage pulls at your heart with a resounding yes! - then you have died with Christ. The Spirit of God has caused you to be born again as a child of God who knows that they can only be saved by the merits of the Son of God by His work on the cross. You know you can only have the desire to live for His glory because He rose from the dead, having taken you with Him to walk in newness of life.

You can only take these truths to heart if you have known the grace of God in Christ Jesus to cause you to desire Him. Jesus Christ offers freely to all sinners to come to Him in order to receive new life in Him, to receive forgiveness for their sins, and to grow in maturity in Him. The Philippians mindset means nothing to someone who has not been born again. For those who have never known what it means to be regenerated, perhaps by the grace of God the Philippians mindset has stirred a desire in your heart to live in such a way.

For anyone who is encouraged by the wisdom in this passage, but who has not known what it means to cast all your hope for forgiveness and salvation from the wrath you deserve on Jesus Christ and His death on the cross- run to Christ now! Put all your faith in Him and end the war you have had with God all your life. Submit yourself to the Lordship of His Son. Turn from your sins and determine to live your life for the prize of the upward call in Christ Jesus.

Chapter Eight

Rejoice in the Lord always. Again I will say, rejoice! Let your gentleness be known to all men. The Lord is at hand. Be anxious for nothing, but in everything by prayer and supplication, with thanksgiving, let your requests be made known to God; and the peace of God, which surpasses all understanding, will guard your hearts and minds through Christ Jesus. -Philippians 4:4-7

What do experts say is the most common mental illness in the United States? They call it *anxiety*. 40 million adults suffer from what could be called clinical anxiety, according to a report in 2018. By 2020, the market for benzodiazepines, the drug family which includes Xanax, Librium, Valium and Ativan had been expected to reach 3.8 billion dollars in the U.S. alone.[31]

In reality, anxiety is just a common biproduct of the effects of sin throughout history and all the uncertainties it brings in the realms of health, safety, finances, and spirituality. The church in Philippi struggled with anxiety as well. It would seem that many in the early church did. Would you not be tempted to grow anxious with all of the variables that being a follower of Jesus brought to the table in the first century?

In fact, the great apostle who helped bring the church of Philippi into existence was writing this letter to them while in chains himself! Was Paul immune to temptations to grow anxious while he was in prison? Certainly not. Likewise, many in the early church, no doubt, lived under the constant threat of imprisonment and death and destitution from being excluded from the marketplace and the guilds. To be sure, the

---

[31] https://www.cnbc.com/2018/08/02/antianxiety-drugs-fuel-the-next-deadly-drug-crisis-in-us.html

early believers were often tempted to grow anxious and fall prey to fits of severe anxiety.

Anxiety is a very real threat to mental health in any culture in any given time period in history. Paul was unable to point people to benzodiazepines in the first century, and this is not the place to discuss mental illness and medication. Let it just be said in passing that medication can be a legitimate tool in a Christian's life to help stabilize their mental health. On the other hand, there is also the very real suspicion today that many people are being either overly medicated or given medication to mask issues of the heart that should really be dealt with in Biblical counseling. But this still does not rule out the need for psychiatric medications in many cases.

Everyone reading this book has struggled with the temptation to grow anxious at some point. The Holy Spirit has placed here in Phil 4:4-7 several quick injunctions (something Paul does quite often), a tightly packed grouping of imperatives which here in Philippians bring the believer to a place of peace that will guard their heart and mind.

How can we fight and battle against and squelch anxiety in our hearts and minds? We need to fill the mind with something other than the spiraling thoughts of despair and irrational hopelessness that consumes it. When you grow anxious there is no hope in trying to empty your mind of everything. You have to fill it with what these injunctions are calling for.

You have probably noticed already that Paul says to rejoice, he says to be gentle or forbearing, and he says to pray. It seems from the passage that engaging in these mindsets will cause anxiety to flee and the peace of God to set a guard around our hearts and our minds. Rejoicing, gentleness (or not clinging to your own rights), and prayer- yet again, another list of self-help techniques that will bring us mental health.

No! No… rather, the key to this series of tightly packed imperatives and the key to driving away anxiety in our hearts, is really only the *one* thing that this passage is pointing us to. You see, woven like a master thread throughout all of these imperatives is the only thing that can cause anxiety to flee. The only *one* who can cause anxiety to flee. Look again at what the passage says: "Rejoice *in the Lord*......Let your gentleness be known to all men *the Lord is at hand*. Be anxious for nothing, but in everything by prayer and supplication with thanksgiving let your requests be made known *to God*..... and the peace *of God*, which surpasses all understanding will guard your hearts and minds *through Christ Jesus*." The Philippians mindset, in this passage, is really to get our minds on *God*, through Christ Jesus. "You will keep him in perfect peace, whose mind is stayed on You" (Isa. 26:3).

All of our troubles in life, when it comes to the mind, when it comes to anxieties, when it comes to warped perspectives on our circumstances, when it comes to worry and despair and discouragement- they all come about because we are not beholding God as He says He is in the eyes of our hearts and minds. Our gaze upon the beauty of the Lord has to often been distracted to gaze on the violent waves of the turmoil of this life. We have locked our sights on the problems of our plight, we have fixed the grip of our minds upon the impossibilities of our situation, we have focused upon the physical pain and the sickening emotions that everything around us whips up time and time again because sin runs amuck and wickedness prowls the earth.

Paul gives us 3 remedies, 3 ways to get our focus and to get our perspectives back on God Almighty, back onto the omnipotent creator who decreed whatsoever comes to pass, back upon your Redeemer King who has providentially orchestrated your circumstances for your good- for your best- to conform you into the image of the Lord Jesus Christ.

We are to rejoice in the Lord, first of all. Second, we are to be gentle before the Lord, and third we are to pray to the Lord. With all three of these remedies, the key is that *God* is part of the remedy. God is able, He is King on high, and none of your circumstances are beyond him, not even your constant struggles with anxiety.

Rejoice in the Lord

First of all, Rejoice in the Lord. Be happy in God. Worship Jesus Christ. Adore your savior. Press into His presence. Hunger for His Fellowship. Desire to know Him and to sit at His feet.

Christians should daily take delight in the fact that the Father loved them before the foundation of the world, that the Son of God died for their sins and rose again from the dead giving them new life and victory over sin, and that the Spirit of God has been sent to dwell within them and to cry out from within the depths of their souls, "Abba, Father!" Rejoice in the Lord. Rejoice in God.

This is a mental effort many times. We are not always happy. Paul is not saying to always be happy here. Did you get that? Paul is not an unrealistic, super-idealistic, positive-thinking, name it and claim it kind of guy! Read 2 Corinthians. Paul acknowledged that he sometimes despaired of life, he was perplexed, he was sorrowful at times. Show me a Christian who always has a smile on their face, even at a tragic funeral, and I will show you someone people think is weird. There is a time to mourn, the Bible says. We are to weep with those who weep. The entire corpus of the Psalms is written by men who continually cried out to the Lord for help and mercy, in desperation and anxiety.

So, what is Paul saying here in Philippians? Rejoice *in the Lord*. Always. When you turn your thoughts towards God, are you considering him in bitterness, in disgust, in hatred? Do you mock God? Do you blaspheme his name? No, when you consider the Lord, you are to rejoice in Him. You worship Him, you delight in Him. This can be done in the middle of a funeral and while you drive home after being fired from your job. It is the regenerated soul's looking to its redeemer in delight over who He is. It is to be glad that God is God, that He is Sovereign. It is to delight that He is the one who puts kings in authority and is the father of the fatherless.

Rejoicing in the Lord is thinking about God the way the Bible describes Him. It is to consider God as God, in His fullness, in His beauty, in His *ability*! It is to take our thoughts captive to the obedience of Christ and rest our hearts on the fact that God is a very present help in time of need. Rejoice in the living God! Rejoice in the redeeming God! Rejoice in the God of glory, the God of creation, the God of election and promise! Paul is calling the Philippians to always be turning their thoughts upon God and who He says He is. Rejoice in the Lord always.

The point is to continually, always, be turning our minds and hearts away from anxious thoughts and distracted thoughts towards a comprehension of who God is and to rejoice in the magnificence we begin to behold in Him in our mind's eye. Sin wants to paint blackout paint over our memories of God. Sin will mar and tweak the glory of God we have previously seen in Scripture or heard preached on a Sunday morning. The apostle tells us to always rejoice *in the Lord*. Take the time to order your perspective on your situation in light of who God really is.

How much time do we spend fretting on our circumstances versus how much time we spend worshiping God and thinking about how wonderful God is, about how able he is to do exceedingly abundantly above all we can ask or think? How much time do we spend rejoicing in who God is compared to how much effort we spend at nursing over our complaints and our worries and our bitterness?

Furthermore, how much time do we spend thinking about God as He *really* is? Do we just cry out to God as a sort of concept we know we can get help from? Are we crying out to God? Or are we crying out to *God*, as He reveals Himself to be?

John MacArthur in his commentary quotes A.W. Tozer in his book, *The Knowledge of the Holy* as saying the following:

> What comes into our minds when we think about God is the most important thing about us. The history of mankind will probably show that no people has ever risen above its religion, and man's spiritual history will positively demonstrate that no religion has ever been greater than its idea of God. Worship is pure or base as the worshiper entertains high or

low thoughts of God. For this reason the gravest question before the Church is always God Himself, and the most portentous fact about any man is not what he at a given time may say or do, but what he in his deep heart conceives God to be like. We tend by a secret law of the soul to move toward our mental image of God. This is true not only of the individual Christian, but of the company of Christians that composes the Church. Always the most revealing thing about the Church is her idea of God, just as her most significant message is what she says about Him or leaves unsaid, for her silence is often more eloquent than her speech. She can never escape the self-disclosure of her witness concerning God. Were we able to extract from any man a complete answer to the question, 'What comes into your mind when you think about God?' We might predict with certainty the spiritual future of that man.[32]

Gentle Before the Lord

Our first remedy to anxiety is to rejoice in the Lord. Our second remedy is to be gentle before the Lord. Verse 5: "Let your gentleness be known to all men. The Lord is at hand." The ESV reads, "Let your reasonableness be known to everyone." The word for "gentleness" or "reasonableness" could also be "equity" or "fairness". Some translate this as a forbearing spirit. William Hendricksen translates it as "Big-heartedness". He says, "For big-heartedness one may substitute any of the following: forbearance, yieldedness, geniality, kindliness, gentleness, sweet reasonableness, considerateness, charitableness, mildness, magnanimity, generosity."[33] There is not a single word in English that can convey this Greek word, but these all together give the sense of it. It is the idea of not looking out for your own interests but looking out for the interests of others that we considered in an earlier part of this book.

---
[32] John MacArthur. *The MacArthur New Testament Commentary, Philippians* (Moody Press, 2001), 274
[33] William Hendricksen. *The New Testament Commentary, Philippians* (Baker Academic, 2007), 193

This is the idea that you yield your rights, that you do not push yourself forward. You rejoice in the exaltation of others. You have resolved the fact that this whole thing was never about you in the first place, and you have determined to let the Lord have his way with you as His slave.

It is gentleness *before the Lord*. Our text links the idea of big heartedness with the phrase: "the Lord is at hand". Remember, God is the master thread through all of these imperatives. We are to continually consider the fact that at any moment we will be standing before the King of glory to give an account of the things we have done in the body.

Some Christians have accomplished much for the kingdom of God. Maybe they have been a pastor who has had far reaching influence over other churches and missions. They have written books and they have preached incredible sermons. But all the while, perhaps they have relished in their power and influence, and maybe they have squashed others to maintain it. They have done big things, but they have not been big-hearted, perhaps.

Unfortunately, the church of Jesus Christ is filled with pastors and workers and servants who hold grudges against each other and suspicions of each other and they hold envy and jealousy for each other. They will do whatever it takes (as long as they can keep appearing godly to others while doing it) to gain influence and to remain in the front of everything that is going on.

But you see, the Lord is at hand. This should strike fear in us. The first shall be last and the last shall be first. Do you always have a hankering for being first? Soon you will stand before the Lord and give an account. Rather, be big- hearted and yield to others. Relinquish your bent to be in the front, to push your name forward. "But, how can I be a leader? I'm called to be a leader!" some might say at this point. I fear that too many of us have a warped idea of what a leader is. We see a little kid bossing everyone around on the playground and we say, "Wow, he's a born leader."

A true leader is big-hearted and generous. Remember Jesus? Was He not a leader? Was He not the *ultimate* leader? How did He treat the disciples? What was all that foot washing stuff about anyways? The Lord is at hand and we will soon stand before him. Will our works and good deeds we bring to his feet just be ashes by the time we get there? Burned to nothing because they were done in the flesh during this life?

Now how does this help us with anxiety? Because our worries and anxieties often center around the fact that we are desiring our own rights. We think we deserve this or that, we think we should not be in this or that circumstance, or we grow anxious because our own reputation is on the line. Many times, our worries are because someone else is messing up our lives, someone else is being annoying or is being hostile to us.

But we are to be big-hearted in all this. We are to yield. "They'll walk all over me if I do that!" you might say. I wonder if they actually will? How much can you afford to be walked over? Is it a matter of someone taking away your resources to leave you in distress, or to really abuse you in some way, or to cause harm to one of your children, or something to that effect? Of course, I am not saying yield to *that* degree. But what measure of sweet reasonableness can you display in your given situation? Do you need to go toe-to-toe with this person? Or can you let go? Can you even be big-hearted in the situation and allow them the attention and awards they seem to be seeking? Will it cost you really that much to do so in the scheme of things? Will it cost you when you stand before the Lord? To be big-hearted?

To yield to a situation in kindness and generosity can often be such a sweet release from anxiety. Maybe there are some reading this who are always anxious about their finances. They feel they never have anything to give to the kingdom of God. They feel they are not able to give tithes and offerings. Maybe for this person a little more big-heartedness in their finances will cause a release of anxiety in their life. Of course, this is an encouragement to worship through giving. We do not want to abuse the poor or the afflicted or desire anyone to give money to the kingdom in a way that they are neglecting providing for their family and their way to make a living.

Some might just have an anxious personality that is so caught up in worries and anxieties all the time. If you are such a person, I hope you have known the sweetness and joy and release from care that being big-hearted and loving towards others and concerning yourself with other peoples' needs has brought to you at times. It feels good to be kind-hearted. It is a balm to the soul to be sweetly reasonable towards others. To be gentle. And the Lord is at hand! Is the King going to commend us for how well we worried and how concerned we were all the time about everything? Or will he look at how we yielded to other people's interests?

This is a catalyst to cast off anxiety: to realize that God Himself is going to consider whether or not we were big-hearted, or whether we were curved inward upon ourselves all the time in fretful anxieties. You see the master thread again: it is to consider God, to consider that we will soon be standing before Him. You are not going to be worried in glory, that is for sure. The Lord is at hand. Allow Him to enlarge your heart, and to give you peace.

Pray to the Lord

Our third remedy is that we are to pray to the Lord. Verse 6: "Be anxious for nothing, but in everything by prayer and supplication with thanksgiving, let your requests be made known to God." Here we see this group of imperatives coming to its climax. Paul is summing up everything here by just stating it bluntly: Be anxious for nothing!

Let go, dear Christian. Let go of your anxious grip upon the worries of your life. You have spent enough of your time in anxieties, in worrying, in fretting. What good has it ever done to your soul? Has your worrying ever enabled you to escape from difficulties and dangers?

If you are one who is a worrier, you need to embrace something. You need to embrace this concept: God is going to continually throughout your life bring in providences that you will be tempted to worry about. God is directing you to travel upon the rough road of this life because He wants to destroy the idols of your heart. Our worries and our sinful anxieties are usually the result of us trusting in idols, rather than in the living God. God is going to continually bring in providences that will be His finger, as it were, pressing you where you are most tender, where your precious idols lie in the bosom of your heart.

If your tendency is to cherish the idols of peace, of financial stability, of health, of your own children or your family, of your own reputation- whatever it is- God is going to test you in this area over and over again. I would say, more than likely, that even if we begin to gain the victory in trusting God when difficulties arise, we will be tested over and over again in these areas for the rest of our lives.

Now instead of growing anxious over this reality, instead of worrying about how we are going to endure a life traveling on the rough roads of difficult providences- we are to instead listen to the Spirt of God encourage us through Paul to let go of our grip on these idols that cause us to fret and to grow anxious, and to turn to the God of glory and live a lifestyle of prayer to Him.

We are to turn away from gritting our teeth in repetitious pondering, over and over again, about the things that trouble us, and to turn to the Lord in prayer. We are to make our request known *to God*. Remember, it is not just that we are to pray. People often tell me in different counseling situations, "I prayed about this. I have been praying, but I am still struggling with what to do." We can pray according to biblical patterns, and with a knowledge that we are praying to the God of the Bible, and we can say our prayers and finish with an "amen", and all the while we never met with God! We never really *prayed*! We did not pray in such a way that we got ourselves into a mindset that was truly worshiping God for *who he says he is*, praying in such a way that our eyes of faith truly beheld the living God. To pray until we were truly praying![34]

The Puritans talked about this: to pray until you really pray. Not to just express flowery words, or beautiful poetic prayers. But to pray until you *know* you are talking to the God of glory! The Almighty! The

---

[34] A concept declared by many of the Puritans

one for whom *nothing*- NOTHING is impossible! The one who is able to give you victory over your anxieties! The one who can cause you to trust in *Him*, even though the circumstances don't change. Even though the circumstance get worse. Though He slay me, yet I will trust Him![35] Trusting in the God of the Bible. Praying to the living God!

These different descriptions of prayer: *prayer, supplication, thanksgiving, requests-* are not meant to be a list of different ways to pray. Moises Silva in his commentary writes,

> Paul uses four different words in reference to prayer… this variety does not indicate an attempt to identify four discrete types of, or elements in, prayer. Apart from the occurrence of *eucharistia-* which certainly refers to the distinct aspect of thanksgiving and which appears to receive some emphasis- the variation has a stylistic motive… the real significance of this stylistic richness is not what it says about the theological components of prayer (or the psychological makeup of human beings) but rather about the great importance that Paul attaches to the believer's prayer life.[36]

You see, the point is: engage with God. Do it with an overall thankfulness, yes, but pray *to Him*. Now, God can answer your prayers with a "no". He may not give you what you ask. But if you are making your requests known to *Him*, if you are engaging in becoming enveloped in the presence of the King of the universe, engaged in fellowship with the Lord of Lords, knowing that you are casting your cares upon His listening ear, then you will be coming away from that time of prayer encouraged with a vision of the God who is able to do exceedingly abundantly above all we can ask or think. You will be encouraged with a vision in your heart that God is able to guide you as the Great Shepherd of the Sheep throughout the entire length of the valley of humiliation, knowing he gives you a

---

[35] Job 13:15
[36] Moises Silva. *Philippians, Baker Exegetical Commentary on the New Testament* (Baker Academic, 2005), 195

song in the night in order for you to behold the stars above as you stand sunken in the pit. You come away from such an experience of praying to the living God with your anxieties having been chased away. You come away with the peace of God.

It is a peace which surpasses understanding. Your circumstances have not changed, but yet you have this peace that God is going to get you through and that He is going to uphold you with His righteous right hand. He is going to be with you in the furnace of affliction, "and the peace of God, which surpasses all understanding, will guard your hearts and minds through Christ Jesus."

This is not just some feeling of peace that God gives you, but the peace *of God*. It is a peace that has been given to you because you have immersed yourself in a vision of the Almighty. "Of God", in the Greek is in the genitive case which is kind of like the case of possession. When you say, "Mary's bible"- Mary would be in the genitive case in Greek. But there are different kinds of genitives. Here in Philippians 4:7, the genitive is what we call the genitive of production. You see *God* produces this peace.

It is not so much that God produces the peace and gives it to you as a separate gift. It is rather that, by immersing wholly in prayer to *God*: the thought of God, the pondering of God, the rejoicing in the Lord, the being gentle before God, the seeking of God- this fills your mind with God's greatness. It is knowing a deep vision of God in your heart. This is what produces peace in your soul. God produces peace in you. But you have to grasp Him by faith, engaging in these 3 remedies to get your mindset to see God as He is and for Him to produce peace in your soul.

Again, this is the master thread in this passage: *God*. The God of peace. Get your thoughts on God, which will bring you peace and calm in your troubled soul. Do not just pray a polished prayer and say "Amen" and expect peace to be given to you. Pray until you pray. Draw near to God. Consider Him, His ways, His power, His glory! Put your faith in *Him*! Believe He is a very present help in times of trouble. Do not just acknowledge what that means in the English language but believe it in the depths of your soul!

It was said of Martyn Lloyd- Jones, that great preacher in London during the 20th century, that one suddenly felt a calmness, a stilling of one's heart when you were around him. The pastoral prayers he prayed during the Sunday morning services at Westminster Chapel were usually between 10 and 15 minutes long. And many people who came to hear him preach would say that they were often so helped by the presence of God during the prayer, that they could have left the chapel at that point even before the preaching.

Now I believe all of this was because the Doctor, as they called him, was often filled with the peace of God, and it reverberated into those around Him. He had the peace of God, because he was filled with a vision of *Who God is as He says He is*. He rejoiced *in the Lord*, He was big-hearted *before God*, and He prayed until He prayed. He Prayed *to God*. And this peace of God filled Martyn Lloyd-Jones and surrounded His ministry.

When God meets with us, we must be still and know that He is God. But the Bible says, "draw near to God, and He will draw near to you" (James 4:8). Do you want to be a man or woman filled with the peace of God? Of course, you do! Fill your heart up with God. Stop playing with those precious idols you so foolishly depend upon. The Lord is at hand. We must live *Coram Deo*, before the face of God. Not a God we know only in theological precision and correctness, but a God we *know*! The living God who is worthy of all our praise.

And this peace of God can only come through the Lord Jesus Christ, as the end of verse 7 implies. You cannot hope to draw near to a holy God, apart from having your sins cast away from God's sight through the death of Christ on the cross- the death He died as a living shield from the wrath of God against our sins. You cannot pray to God, unless you approach Him through Jesus Christ, the great Mediator between sinners and a holy God.

Only by His merits can
The sinner approach, nor can he stand
Before the Holy God above

We now desire since Christ's love
Caused Him to die upon the tree
To make us holy, you and me
So, while we walk upon earth's sod
We can have the peace of God.

Chapter Nine

Finally, brethren, whatever things are true, whatever things are noble, whatever things are just, whatever things are pure, whatever things are lovely, whatever things are of good report, if there is any virtue and if there is anything praiseworthy- meditate on these things. The things which you learned and received and heard and saw in me, these do, and the God of peace will be with you. – Philippians 4:8,9

As we consider the Philippians mindset in this present passage, we note that our mental key word is the word translated in English as "meditate". We hear a lot about meditation these days. Usually, in our culture, the idea of meditation carries with it an Eastern-mystical kind of sense, where we are trying to calm our minds, empty our minds, to focus our thoughts onto something peaceful, something tranquil. Many people see no harm in directing their mindset toward emptying themselves of all intrusive thoughts and of focusing on scenes of serenity.

However, there are dangerous forms of meditation that have been taught and followed throughout the history of the world. These forms of meditation can be found in many false religions and in forms of witchcraft and spiritism. The kind of tamed down version of it all that is popular in America today, is again, to quiet the mind and to focus on tranquility.

Now, in and of itself, trying to calm down and cease from being anxious is a good thing. It can be a good thing to try to quiet oneself and to control your breathing in such a way that you avoid something like a panic attack or hysteria. There is nothing inherently wrong in thinking about a calm lake or an ocean or imagining peaceful scenes of tranquility in your mind in order to get away from the day's confusion and oppression. But the meditation Paul is describing here in the book of Philippians has nothing to do with any of these kinds of thought processes we have been talking about.

Really, these verses flow out of the passage we considered in the last chapter in verses 4-7, where the apostle gives three God-saturated remedies of how to cast out anxiety and to know the peace of God in one's heart and mind. To get rid of anxiety, ultimately, we are not to *empty* our minds, but to *fill* our minds and our hearts with a vision of God.

And here in verses 8 and 9, that thought continues. There were so many things vying for the Philippians' attention, so many temptations to grow anxious, so many threats and fears around them. Physical weakness and disease, the threat of persecution, abuse by the Romans, the possibility of being cast out of the marketplace, dangers of famine and weather- all of this entailed that the road of life was rough in the first century for Christians.

Now Paul directs them towards a further way to be mentally healthy. Another aspect of the Philippians mindset: To meditate. Not in the way that one floats in some mystic, almost trance-like state above a vision of a calm ocean, but to meditate in such a way that one's mind and heart is *filled* with good things.

The Greek word for meditate here, *Logizesthe*, has imbedded within it a form of a word from where we get the English word "logic". *Logizesthe* means to count, to reckon, to calculate, to take into account, to credit, to place into one's account, to consider, to think, to suppose, to evaluate, to look upon as, to class, to maintain, to claim, to think on, to reflect upon.[37]

Kittel tells us that this Greek word had common to its sense the idea of an act of thought according to strict logical rules, such as in commercial dealings for either charging up a debt or estimating the value of an

---

[37] These definitions are all from the Lexicon located in the UBS Greek New Testament, Reader's Edition.

object.³⁸ So really, the idea of meditating here is calculating, adding up, logically determining the worth and value of good things.

We are to think upon noble, just, pure, lovely things, things of good report, virtuous and praiseworthy things in such a way that we actually logically calculate the value of these things in our lives. We evaluate the weight these things will have in eternity, and the way God is glorified in them.

It is not that we are to simply run across something good within our memories. We are to reflect upon these things in a way that we calculate the goodness of God in our lives and in the world around us. To borrow a worn illustration: we look at that glass that is half full. We calculate how glorious it is that we have access to water in that glass and that we can quench our thirst as well as help nourish someone else who is thirsty with that half full cup. We rejoice because we know the glass was filled up previously from a water source that we have access to continually. We praise God for giving mankind the mind and the gifts to be able to blow glass and create cups that can hold liquid. These are all ways we can meditate on a glass that is half full.

Now, this list of good things here in verse 8 is not meant to be an exhaustive list of the kinds of things Paul is calling us to meditate upon. Paul is only whetting our thoughts. But let us consider them each in turn.

First, whatever things are true. "True" is the Greek word *alethe*. This carries with it the idea of something not hidden or concealed. It is the actual occurrence, the fact about something.³⁹ In this world we are surrounded with lies and deceptions. The whole world lies under the sway of the wicked one, the apostle John tells us. In this world where people act in deception, where politicians are as slick as grease, and where the economy depends upon heartless advertising designed for one thing (to get you to buy!), we need to meditate, to calculate, to reckon, and to ponder what is true.

---

[38] Gerhard Kittel, ed. *Theological Dictionary of the New Testament, Vol. IV* (Eerdmans, 1967), 284
[39] Gerhard Kittel, ed. *Theological Dictionary of the New Testament, Vol. I* (Eerdmans, 1964), 238

This means thinking often about the world we live in on the Bible's terms, and not on the terms of what the culture is telling us is true. We are to meditate on the fact that the world is the way it is because of sin. The Bible tells us this is the true reason for the problems in the world. Why is anything uncomfortable ultimately happening to us? Why does the economy go up and down? Why are there wars and disease? Why is there sorrow and death? Ultimately, it is because sin has entered the world. And we need to often consider this. This is what is true.

When we fall into the trap of thinking things are just happening because it is a chaotic world, a world of chance, or a world of people who have not reached actualization or understood properly positive thinking, then we are becoming deceived about the truth about the world, and therefore we are becoming distracted from the *one* remedy to this world's problems.

We need to think upon the truth that we are engaged in a spiritual warfare, considering the fact that there is a devil, and demons, and that they are seeking to destroy souls. But, in all this we need to also think about the one true God who rules over all, and who decrees whatsoever comes to pass. We need to meditate upon the truth that God is in control of all things and that He is trustworthy. We need to ponder the truth that God created the heavens and the earth and that we are not descended from apes or amoebas. We need to think upon the truth that our neighbor's greatest need is forgiveness of sin available only in Christ Jesus. We are to consider that the gospel is the true good news and that it is the power of God unto salvation. We should chew upon the fact that the Biblical historical account is accurate and true. God *did* create Adam and Eve. He *did* deliver Israel from Egypt. He *did* part the Red Sea and gave manna from heaven. His Son *did* become a human being and was born of a virgin and died on the cross and rose again for our justification. We should be dwelling upon the truth that Christ is coming again and that He will judge the living and the dead.

Whatever is true. We are being bombarded with different narratives from our culture as to what is true. The world says that whatever you think is true is true. But the word of God says that Jesus is the way, the truth and the life (Jn. 14:6), and no one comes to the Father but through Him. That is true truth, as Francis Schaeffer would have called it. We desperately need to look at the world around us through the lens of truth, through the lens of the Bible. And we need to do so reckoning and pondering what that means for us and the people we love and the people we work with. We need to calculate what that means for people who have never heard the gospel, and for those who have grown up in absolute spiritual darkness, deep in the recesses of the 10/40 window (the latitude/ longitude where the greatest number of unreached people live in the world).

We also need to think about the truth that the good news of Jesus Christ is spreading like wildfire throughout the world. What the news does not report to us through TV and the internet and the radio is that the Spirit of God is working and moving and that His word cannot be chained. We need to think of the truth that not only is an incredible revival is going on south of the United States, but actually a reformation. In Latin America alone, the number of people becoming Protestant Christians each year is staggering. We need to calculate and reckon with the truth that the gospel is the power of God unto salvation, that God is saving souls and that He is completely capable and able to do it and to continue doing it. Christians should calculate what it means that God hears and answers prayers according to His will. Whatever we ask the Father in Jesus' name He will accomplish.

Meditate on these things! Meditate on whatever is true. Whatever actually is fact. Secondly, we are to meditate on whatever things are noble. "Noble" is the Greek word *semna*. It means honorable, whatever is worthy of reverence.[40] We think mostly here of people and of people's actions, noble things people have done, and the ways honor is reflected in different peoples' character.

This is so edifying to do: to meditate on the noble qualities in other men and women of God. This is why it is so good to always be reading

---

[40] Gerhard Kittel, ed. *Theological Dictionary of the New Testament, Vol. VII* (Eerdmans, 1971), 195

through a biography, especially Christian biographies. We know that no man, woman, boy or girl is perfect or without sin, but many times biographies help us meditate and help us to reckon upon the honorable aspects to a person's character so that we can let our own minds soak in their mindsets.

This is one of the reasons why I think I love C.H. Spurgeon's writings so much. There is a nobility of character that seems to emanate from his writings. Here is a sampling of an address to his pastors who had been sent out from the pastor's college:

> Brethren, let us look well to our own steadfastness in the faith, our own holy walking with God. Some say that such advice is selfish; but I believe that, in truth, it is not selfishness, but a sane and practical love of others which leads us to be mindful of our own spiritual state. Desiring to do its level best, and to use its own self in the highest degree to God's glory, the true heart seeks to be in all thing right with God. He who has learned to swim has fostered a proper selfishness, for he has thereby acquired the power of helping the drowning. With the view of blessing others, let us covet earnestly the best blessings for ourselves.[41]

Another man of God, whose biography I love to read, and who I feel displayed a nobility of character, was Martyn Lloyd Jones. Listen to this sample from a letter he wrote to his daughter Elizabeth when she was in Oxford. Iain Murray says of this letter in his biography of Lloyd-Jones that previously, Elizabeth "had clearly written something about the view which was tending to be adopted by herself and others in the Oxford Inter-Collegiate Union on attendance at their colleges' chapels. There was criticism of the chapel services, especially of the hymns sung."[42]

Here is how Martyn Lloyd-Jones replied to his daughter:

---

[41] Charles Spurgeon. *An All-Round Ministry* (Pilgrim Publications, 1983), 232
[42] Iain Murray. *D.M. Lloyd Jones, The Fight of Faith* (The Banner of Truth Trust, 1990), 176

> Your attitude is not one that I can commend… Your duty is to show that your views and beliefs lead to a higher and finer type of Christian life and living. Then that will lead others to speak to you and to enquire as to your secret. To start a division on odd points and to raise difficulties especially in a matter like that of hymns seems to me to be the worst possible approach. It gives the impression that you are intolerant and that you regard yourselves as heresy hunters. Your duty it seems to me is to attend the services. If you find you cannot sing a hymn, just refrain from doing so… You must beware of falling into what appears to be the common evangelical trap and snare namely an over-punctiliousness about matters that are relatively unimportant and a tendency to neglect more vital matters such as love and charity….[43]

When we read the letters and the biographies of these great men of God, we can steep ourselves in mindsets which displayed honorable and revered ways of thinking, speaking and acting. Have you ever caught someone acting in a way that really impressed you in this way? Have you gone away from encountering something like that and meditated on what it means to act in that manner? What does it take to bring our own character in line with such noble ways?

I think so often, especially for men, that we can play out and imagine in our mind's eye doing something heroic. We rehearse what we would do if we saw someone trying to kidnap somebody. Or we think of what we would do if someone came into the church building with a gun. We replay these scenes over and over in our minds. That is all for heroics. Do we do the same thing regarding noble character? Do we spend time mediating on whatever is noble?

Perhaps you have gotten into a disagreement with your wife. Do you go away rehearsing in your mind how you can go back and express your mind and tell her how she was wrong and point out her selfishness to her

---

[43] Ibid.

and express how she has wronged you over and over again in the past? Do you spend time fuming in your mind about what you will say or do next time the same issue comes up between the two of you?

Or, instead, are you meditating on what would be honorable to do in that situation? What would Jesus do? What would Paul do? What would some of these great missionaries we read about have done in that situation? How can I act when this comes up again in a way that my wife or my husband will actually have to confess that I am honorable and noble in my character? (Noble does not mean snooty or self-righteous!)

This Greek word for "noble" actually means majesty and greatness as well. We have been thinking in terms of character, but really, Kittel tells us this could mean the inner majesty of things or the outward greatness of things. Again, Kittel tells us a thing is *semnos* if the signs of a higher order may be detected in it.[44] So it is not just in people's character we sense this kind of nobility, this sense of higher order, this trace of God's Spirit in people, but we sense nobility in the outward majesty of things which are around us.

We see this in the blazing sunsets on the horizon of the ocean, and we see it in the immensity of the Grand Canyon. But we also sense it in the beauty and intricacy of the eyes of men and animals, in the design of the circulatory system, and in the power of the horse. In all these things we detect the majesty, the nobility of our Creator God.

We sense it also in the art and architecture that people, made in the image of God are able to create and to produce. Yes, the Taj Mahal is an Islamic building, but we see the nobility of the image of God reflected in its majesty and magnificence. Some of the airplanes that men have manufactured over the last 100 years have transmitted a kind of majesty in their lines of design and in their power and agility. And we are to meditate on these things! Whatever is noble. Calculate the majesty you see in people's character, in the colors and shapes of creation all around you, be they man-made or natural.

---

[44] Gerhard Kittel, ed. *Theological Dictionary of the New Testament, Vol. VII* (Eerdmans, 1971), 193

Paul goes on to say, "whatever things are just." The word translated "just" is the Greek word *dikaia*. It means conforming to the standard, will, or character of God. It means upright, righteous, good, proper; to be in a right relationship with God; fair, honest, innocent.[45] We are to reckon upon things that are just and how justice can be distributed throughout society. We cannot just think of court justice here. Think of living in a right relationship to God.

How can you live honestly before God? What needs to change in your life, in the way you work for your employer, in the way you act towards your children, in the ways you sing during the Lord's Day? Are our hearts honest before God? Is our conscience clear?

Now, if we are indeed truly honest and fair before God, you and I must confess right now that we have failed to meditate upon and to emulate just, righteous living before God. However, we are not to stagger in condemnation over this. As we consider the Philippians mindset we will, of course, be convicted and will see how far we fall short many times. Yet, we are not to stumble in a discouraged paralysis!

Run to the Just One, the Righteous One, who was crucified for you! Do we count the blood of Christ a common thing? Or will we embrace Him by faith, confess our sins, and run under the fountain of blood that remains open and flowing for all of our sins? "He has shown you, oh man, what is good and what the Lord requires of you… but to do justly, and to love mercy, and to walk humbly with your God" (Mic. 6:8). We are to humbly run to His mercy and believe in His mercy which is always available to us in Christ every time we fail to do justly.

But one thing that is just, one thing that is righteous, is to get back up after you fall. Proverbs 24:16, "For a righteous man may fall seven times, and rise again, but the wicked shall fall by calamity." Whatever things are just? Whatever things are righteous? What kinds of things does that mean we are to think about? It means thinking about running to Jesus, of repenting and confessing our sins, of crying out to Him for power

---

[45] Gerhard Kittel, ed. *Theological Dictionary of the New Testament, Vol. II* (Eerdmans, 1964), 211-219

and grace to get back up and follow Him. It means thinking about how God was just and at the same time the justifier of sinners on the cross of calvary!

"But to do justly, and to love mercy, and to walk humbly with your God." In order to think about righteous living and about living with a right relationship to God, we have to go low, we have to be humble, and we have to run to mercy and forgiveness in Jesus. We are to loathe our own sin and to hate what it has done to us and to others, hating what sin has done to the ones we love. We are called to hate what sin has done to this world. Therefore, meditate on the fact that all wickedness will be dealt with on that Day. Justice will reign in the kingdom to come.

Children who have been abused will be vindicated. Women who have been abused will be vindicated. The poor who have been abused and taken advantage of will be vindicated. Tribes and nations that have been overrun by dictators and vicious armies will be vindicated. And of course, the martyrs of the church will be vindicated. Revelation 6:9,10:

> When He opened the fifth seal, I saw under the altar the souls of those who had been slain for the word of God and for the testimony which they held. And they cried with a loud voice, saying, 'How long, O Lord, holy and true, until You judge and avenge our blood on those who dwell on the earth?

The Lord will take vengeance on His enemies on that Day and it is right and good that He will. It is a terrifying thought, to be sure. But we are to meditate on these things. Calculate what this means. Reckon what this means regarding your witness to this perishing world. Reckon what this means regarding your own salvation: what Justice we all deserve but will never taste! Because of Jesus!

Paul goes on to say, "whatever things are pure." This is the Greek word *agna*. Thayer's lexicon mentions this means to be pure from carnality, chaste, and modest, but the lexicon says that here in Philippians 4:8 it means more along the lines of pure from every fault, immaculate.[46] Both ideas could be implied in our passage, nonetheless.

What are we meditating on in our private moments? Pure things? What is our default meditative position? Is it suspicion, one of paranoia, bitter thoughts, jealous thoughts, lustful thoughts, hateful thoughts, melancholy thoughts? Or are we reckoning upon what it means to think purely and to live purely? And what usually makes us laugh? How often do we laugh out of pure joy, immaculate joy, rather than laughing at someone's expense or at how foolish we think something is?

Our passage says to meditate also on "whatever things are lovely." We are seeing overlapping, similar ideas here. The Greek word for "lovely" is *prospsile*. Thayer's defines it as what is acceptable, what is pleasing.[47] The best way I can imagine this is to simply think about the ways of God. The fruits of the Spirit are a good thing to meditate on in this respect: love, joy, peace, longsuffering, kindness, goodness, faithfulness, gentleness, self-control….. we are to calculate what it means to embrace these ways of God in different situations, in different conversations, with different family members, at different job sites or meetings, on the airplane as we travel, in that confrontation we need to make, in that seeking of forgiveness we have been convicted to do, in stepping forward to serve Christ in that way or in that ministry. God's ways are lovely, they are pleasing. They are beautiful! His ways are higher than our ways and his thoughts higher than our thoughts (Isa. 55:8,9).

Think about, latch on to, something lovely your son or daughter did, something your husband or wife said. Ponder it, think about it. We should overlook the faults and the warts we see in others, and instead zoom in on what is lovely about them. "Well, they said something that was totally rude to me," we think. But look at how they made that sacrifice for someone in the name of Christ. Meditate on *that*…. instead of chewing like a cow does the cud over the offenses they have committed, the faults they have, the ways they do not meet our standards. Stop

---

[46] Joseph H. Thayer. *Thayer's Greek-English Lexicon of the New Testament* (Hendrickson Publishers, 2014), 8

[47] Ibid., 550

shooting around and around in your brain like a pin ball all of the ways which that person seems to parent their children below your standards and your way of doing things. Instead, meditate on how you saw them one afternoon light up with a tear in their eye when they saw that their daughter drew a picture for them in Sunday School. Meditate on *that*. Calculate what that means.

Think about how every Christian in the church will one day be like Jesus. Consider the truth that each believer wants to be like Jesus. We all have that in common as believers. Meditate on that. We are weak, we have fallen seven times, but we keep getting back up again and again and again. Reckon what that means.

Paul starts coming to a crescendo and it seems he is linking all of these ideas together as similar and related to each other. It is, as a whole, a certain way of thinking- a mindset. He says: "whatever things are of good report, if there is any virtue and if there is anything praiseworthy- mediate on these things." "Good report" can mean worthy of praise, the Greek word *euphema*.[48] "Virtue" is the Greek word *arete* which can mean any excellence of a person, an eminent endowment, a virtuous course of thought, moral goodness.[49] Finally, the English word "praise worthy" is the Greek word *epainos*, meaning approbation or commendation.[50] It is as if Paul's words are beginning to melt together in a spirit of worshiping the ways of God. By now we are getting this full-orbed picture of the Philippians mindset. We are beginning to set our thoughts and our thought patterns on high and lofty things, on matters of moral goodness, on ways of virtue and noble-mindedness.

Of course, all of these things we see ultimately in the person of Jesus. He is the lily of the valley. He is the bright and morning star. He is the express image of the Father. He emanates everything true, everything just, everything lovely. And His love for His church and His delight

---

[48] Barabara Aland, Kurt Aland, Johannes Karavidopoulos, Carlo M. Martini, and Bruce Metzger, eds. *The UBS Greek New Testament Reader's Edition with Textual Notes.* (Deutsche Bibelgesellschaft, 2001), 531

[49] Joseph H. Thayer. *Thayer's Greek-English Lexicon of the New Testament* (Hendrickson Publishers, 2014), 73

[50] Ibid., 227

in His children enables all of His goodness, His righteousness, and His virtue to be poured out over our heads in the anointing of His Spirit as He delights to call us His own. As He draws near to us as His beloved Bride, He moves us with desire for Him and His likeness. O, how we long to be like Him, to look upon Him, to gaze upon His beauty!

Look to Jesus, dear Christian. His perfections, His goodness, His truth, His nobility- they are all yours because He bled and died and rose for you. They are ours in Him. Meditate upon that. Think about that. Calculate what that means. And may God grant us His peace.

Chapter Ten

But I rejoiced in the Lord greatly that now at last your care for me has flourished again; though you surely did care, but you lacked opportunity. Not that I speak in regard to need, for I have learned in whatever state I am, to be content: I know how to be abased, and I know how to abound. Everywhere and in all things I have learned both to be full and to be hungry, both to abound and to suffer need. I can do all things through Christ who strengthens me.
-Philippians 4:10-13

So often in life, people think about that one thing they could have or that one way they could live that would truly make them happy. Many of us are driven by the goals we set. Many times, working towards a goal can be a good thing. We should, after all, be seeking to be productive and to accomplish tasks and to move forward in life. But at the same time, so many of us are looking to the end goals which we are striving for as the answer and key to our happiness and contentment.

"Once I retire, then I'll really be at peace and enjoy life," we might think. Or we think, "Once I'm married, then things will be better." Or we determine, "Once we have children, then everything will be in place- we'll be content." "Once I get to that position in work or in the ministry, then things will be alright." How often do we fall into thinking in these kinds of ways?

Again, we are not saying we are not to have goals and to seek to accomplish things and to get to different places in life. But the problem we so often have is that our contentment is often bound up in achieving these goals, in getting these places, and in having "that" amount of money. The problem is that when we place our contentment always in what we do not have, or where we have not gotten to yet, then we end up never being content in life.

Our mental word we see in this passage, our mindset key term, is the word "learned". The one thing we need in life, the one place we need to get to, is not to have kids or wealth or a spouse or a house or to move to this place or that. The one thing we need is to *learn* contentment.

Imagine you never got to this place or that place, or that you never got this thing or that thing which you are desiring. But then imagine that even though you never reached that certain goal, you still, at the same time were content. Through the whole process of trying to reach what you were aiming for, you remained content- content with whether or not you actually got to the place you were seeking to get to. Would you not feel whole and at peace through it all?

Being content is what we actually all really long for. We think this or that will bring us contentment. That is why we want those things or those people or to get to that place. But when we learn to be content in all our circumstances, then we can simply worship God and enjoy God in what He has given to us, no matter if we are abased or if we are abounding.

The word translated "content" in verse 11 is the Greek word *autarkes*. It means "satisfied".[51] Who reading this book does not want to be satisfied in life? How often do we squirm and wriggle under God's mighty hand with dissatisfaction and a longing for peace in our hearts? How often are we not satisfied with God's will in our lives? "For whatever God ordains is right", the old hymn reminds us.

In chapter seven we noted that Paul the apostle was chosen to be a writer of much of the New Testament, not just to tell us what Christ has done for us and how and what we are to do for Him, but that he was chosen as an apostle so we could relate to him. We noted that Paul realized that he had not arrived in life and never would until glory. We can all relate to that. He was the apostle who wrote Romans chapter

---

[51] Barabara Aland, Kurt Aland, Johannes Karavidopoulos, Carlo M. Martini, and Bruce Metzger, eds. *The UBS Greek New Testament Reader's Edition with Textual Notes.* (Deutsche Bibelgesellschaft, 2001), 531

seven, the chapter where he says he did what he did not want to do and he did not do what he wanted to do- all the while explaining his experience as a mature Christian, as an apostle! The apostle who still struggled with sin!

Here again in this passage we are considering, we can relate to Paul the human being, the sinner! We can relate as he says, for I have *learned*! Paul was taught by the Holy Spirit how to do all things through Christ, how to live humbly and to live in prosperity as well. He was taught how to suffer from hunger and yet also how to glorify God in the midst of His abundant provisions. But Paul had to learn this, he had to be taught how to be content. So it is that we can definitely relate to Paul because we are being taught this as well. Just like Paul, we are learning this secret, as it were.

How does the Christian learn to have this mindset? How does the Spirit teach His children how to be content in life? This is how God does it: in case you have not noticed yet, your life can be a bit of a roller coaster. Up and down, up and down it often goes.

Perhaps you have gotten to a place in your job where you have got it down and you feel like you are just coasting along, and you are feeling good in life. Or maybe you finally pay off the mortgage, and you have money in savings to take those vacations you have always wanted to. Or the grandkids are born, and life is rich, life is full. You might have a surgery that seems to have solved a lot of the problems you had- your knee replacement feels great, or you can see now that you have had that cataract surgery. The economy is doing well, and the dollar is strong. You are living in prosperity and things seem on the up and up.

Just when you feel like you have caught your breath, something else goes wrong. Something is reported in the news to cause you anxiety. The pipe underneath the house bursts. Your kids all get the stomach bug. The company threatens layoffs. Your doctor gives you the blood test results. Someone in the family suddenly dies. There is a shock. Or the child is born with a severe disability. Your life has changed. You have such severe carpal tunnel that you can no longer perform your duties at work. There are big ups and downs, and little ups and downs all in between- life is a bit of a roller coaster!

But this is exactly how we learn. To learn contentment, God must take us through the ups and downs. To learn how to be abased and how to abound, we must experience both, to whatever degree. All of your life, God is teaching you to be content. This is what is going on. He is teaching us to be satisfied. It is not that he is teaching us to be immune to pain, suffering, heartache, or loss. But he is teaching us to have an underlying satisfaction in Christ through all of life's ups and downs.

Part of the key to beginning to learn contentment in all our circumstances is first of all embracing the reality that you will be tested in this area over and over again, most likely for the rest of your life. Now that truth causes you to do one of two things: Either you despair of life and retreat into a fit of anxiety, or you run to the shelter of Jesus Christ and cast all your cares and hopes and dependency on Him and Him alone. You see, verse 13 says, I can do all things *through Christ*! Through Christ Who strengthens me. We will speak more on that below.

But we must embrace this reality: that life is filled with ups and downs and comforts and pains and there will always be this kind of ebb and flow in your life. Not only that, but you will always have unreached goals that lie before you. There will always be unfulfilled plans, and places you have not yet arrived in your own strength of character. What we need to learn during these travelling days is how to be *satisfied* despite all of this.

How did Paul learn this? Well, I believe one of the ways he learned this was through saturating himself in the Philippians mindset. All that we have seen so far in the past nine chapters on this topic is how Paul was able to settle into a state of general contentment in his life.

Paul made continual prayerful recollection with joy, confidence, with solidarity and affection for the people of God. He was able to grow in knowledge and discernment in love by identifying goodness, being genuine, and bearing fruit. Assured of his deliverance, Paul knew that to live is Christ and to die is gain and thus he was determined to remain serving the church of Jesus Christ. Paul lived for a unity to be worthy of the gospel, together for the gospel, and he knew he must suffer for the gospel. He loved the beauty of Christian love, the unity of Christian love, the humility of Christian love, and he was inspired by the humility of Christ's love. Paul counted all things loss in order to know Christ personally, to know Christ in power, and to know Christ in suffering. He considered himself as never arriving and he at the same time did not consider anything about himself. In fact, he really only considered one thing in life. Paul rejoiced in the Lord, he was gentle before the Lord, and he continually prayed to the Lord. And finally, Paul meditated- he calculated all of the true, high, and lofty things and ways of God, all of the provisions of Christ, and all of the wonderful ways God's glory is reflected throughout the earth. As Paul lived the Christian life in these mindsets, he was able to draw near to Christ and grow in the grace and knowledge of Christ. He was able to become more and more satisfied in Christ!

Now the mindset we see portrayed throughout the book of Philippians is not exhaustive of all the details of thinking God's thoughts after Him that we see articulated in the word of God. But, as Christians take their thoughts captive to the obedience of Christ by working out their own salvation with fear and trembling and putting on the Lord Jesus Christ and dying to self and praying without ceasing and weeping with those who weep and loving their enemies and setting their minds on things above and forgiving even as Christ has forgiven them- what happens is that the word of God they are meditating on day and night and seeking to work out in their daily thoughts and actions- this word of Truth *sanctifies* the believer! God more and more conforms us into the image of Jesus Christ!

It is like the small, thin thread, which at first is weak and wispy, a tiny insignificant string. Yet, as it is wound together tightly over and over again, it eventually turns into a baseball: hard and solid and able to make an impact. So it is that as we take in the mindsets of the word of God and as we consider and pray into our minds and hearts the Philippians mindset, we will begin to emanate more and more of the peace of God.

Though anxieties threaten within and without, we will be able to exude more and more of contentment and satisfaction, whether we are abased or whether we are abounding.

The Spirit of God is teaching us in the school of Christ how to learn these things. But what we so often do is give up on ever reaching maturity in the Lord. We feel overwhelmed at our own weaknesses. We feel it is too far a journey to get to a place of contentment within the circumstances in which we find ourselves. We feel we will never be a person who displays the peace of God to those around them.

We must remember that part of this mindset is to be confident that He who began a good work in us will complete it, as we saw in chapter one. You see, we can do all these things *through Christ*, who strengthens us! We must walk by faith in the reality that the power of Christ is at work in us!

If you struggle with this thought, you must understand that you may have been believing lies about yourself. If you are a believer then God is at work in you, and He is not going to stop or give up on you! He is achieving His will in your life if you are a Christian. It is time to believe that. This is how we learn contentment. We believe that we can live life through Christ! We trust that Christ is living His life through us! "I have been crucified with Christ; it is no longer I who live, but Christ lives in me; and the life which I now live in the flesh I live by faith in the Son of God, who loved me and gave Himself for me"(Gal. 2:20).

Are you living life through Christ? Are you living by faith in the Son of God? Do you believe that you can do all things through Christ and that He will strengthen you? Or are you just trying to get through each workday, just trying to get to the weekend? When the Lord's Day comes you hear a sermon and say, "Amen", and then forget all about what God spoke to you by Monday morning. Then, you just try to drive your flesh through the week to get to the next weekend and do it all over again.

Have you been born again? Then, Christ lives in you! Live by faith in the Son of God. Believe all that you have in Him and believe that He is going to work in you, through you, this coming week. In the years ahead, He will be working as well. He is going to teach you, to conform you. Believe it! The power of Christ is at work!

You say, "I have not seen many results in myself since I have been a Christian." Now, here is where we must learn the secret art of contentment. This is the kind of thing we have to face. Being bogged down in your sanctification, feeling like you have gotten nowhere, struggling with the same sins you always have, or feeling like you're always in the flesh- is that not a form, a way of being *abased*, of living humbly as our text here says? Is this not a way of suffering hunger, as Paul says? Can we not include this as a season of abasement in our Christian life? Does our text not include this kind of lowly state?

As we are tempted towards depression and laziness in the means of grace when we face the reality that our growth has been stunted as a Christian, it is in these kinds of downs in life that we must begin to learn contentment. It is not that we are just fine with where we are in our lack of growth. But, instead of moaning and groaning and becoming depressed, we instead need to simply put our trust in Jesus Christ. Our moaning and groaning and depression is actually rooted in the fact that we do not really believe Jesus Christ can make us into His own image and cause us to grow. We are not really believing in the power that raised Christ from the dead.

When faced with our shortcomings in our walk with Christ, we are not to grovel and groan in despair, and we do not give up. Instead, we remain content and wait upon Christ and trust in Christ because we are confident that he is at work in us. You can suffer this kind of hunger through Christ who will strengthen you.

We have to learn to do this. And God will keep bringing us low, as it were, to teach us how to get through our stunted season of growth through faith in the Son of God. What begins to happen is that the more you rest and trust in Christ and believe He will live through you, and the more you wait upon Him to cause you to grow and mature, you then begin to grow and mature! You begin to learn to be satisfied in Christ.

We have already said previously in this book that you are never going to arrive in this life. But we can make progress forward. How we do that is by learning to live life through Christ as we suffer hunger and are abased. Do you feel like you can never be the person you want to be? You feel like you always say the wrong things, or that you do foolish things over and over again? You feel like you do not look that great physically and you do not feel like you accomplish much each day? Well, my friend, remember you will never arrive anyway. There will always be the unfulfilled goals in your life. Those things, those positions, that salary- none of it can truly satisfy you.

Fulfillment is living life through Christ. It is when we rest in our precious Lord Jesus and when we realize that He is the only one who truly knows us. It is learning that He is the only one where true riches and treasures lie. He is the only person who can give us the grace to do anything in life for without Him we can do *nothing*! He is the only being who can satisfy us in the midst of the fiery furnace or in the wilderness of famine. Jesus Christ is the bread of life! You cannot live your life without abiding in Him. The Christian life is feeding upon Him day by day, moment by moment. Have you been going elsewhere for your satisfaction, Christian? Have you sought out broken cisterns that can hold no water? Where else can you go, He alone has the words of eternal life!

Therefore, we embrace the reality of ups and downs, and we learn how to live life through Christ, yes, when we are abased. We have been discussing the times and seasons where we are abased and hungry and suffer need.

But what about living in prosperity? What about abounding? "Ah," you might say, "I think I've learned how to be content when I am full- yes, no problem there!" You have all, you suffer no want, everything has been paid off, the kids are married, you got hired for the top position- whatever it is, you have prospered and you are full.

This might be the hardest place to learn contentment, actually. Contentment, true contentment is only found in being satisfied in Christ.

It just so happens that prosperous times can very often distract us from our need for Him. We begin to think we need the stuff, we need the nice house, we need the good economy, we need the health, we need the spouse or the child, in order to remain truly satisfied. That, my friends, is actually a lie.

No, we are not denying there is real grief and sorrow when we suffer losses. Contentment in the pain and tragedy does not numb us from suffering. Note: it is contentment *while* we suffer, we were talking about, suffering through Christ, who gives us strength to get through it.

But we cannot forget that the same goes with being full and abounding. You cannot survive material blessings and providential blessings unless you live by faith in the Son of God. You have to reckon yourself to have been crucified with Christ.

If you are living for the money or the power or the recognition or the safety or the health, then you are in reality committing idolatry! Your idols will eventually leave you empty and in despair. Only Christ can satisfy you, dear reader. The Christian life is going to keep going up and down, up and down as God teaches you and chastises you and conforms you into becoming satisfied in Jesus Christ whether you are abased or whether you abound.

Do you think that is cruel? Do you think it is cruel for God to lead you to the only fountain of water in this whole world-wide desert we call life in this sin-bleached earth? Is it cruel for him to teach you to drink from the fountain of living waters and to cause you to thirst no more? Is that cruel?

We need to be *taught* how to drink from this fountain- that is the problem! That is why we suffer so many times, because we are broken sinners who have everything backwards. We are stuffing our canteens full of sand and dirt! The Spirit of God is teaching us to eat the Bread of Life. "Why cannot he just make me perfect right now?" you might think. He could. Be careful how you complain to God. He could take your life right now, on the way home from work, sometime this year. He could perfect you, Christian- in a moment- and there will be a moment coming when he does! Do not question His timetable.

"Whatever my God ordains is right, holy his will abideth. I will be still what'er he doth and follow where he Guideth." What is that hymn talking about? *Contentment*. Again, contentment here in our text does not mean you will never suffer again. But we "follow where He guideth." "Though dark my road"… we can do all things *through* Jesus Christ.

The world clings to its idols in its times of abasement and in its times of prosperity. It is clinging to them! We cannot go through life without constantly worshiping something. We were designed to walk with a staff. We have to lean on something. The problem is that the world is leaning on an imaginary staff that will suddenly vanish one day like the fantasy it really is, and it will find itself tumbling headlong into Hell itself. There is nothing that can hold our weight over the fires of Hell except the rock of Christ. All other ground is sinking sand.

So why is it that we as Christians return to these broken cisterns? Why do we lean on staffs made of smoke? Why is it we fill our canteens with sand and dirt? "Awake, you who sleep, arise from the dead, and Christ will give you light!" the Scripture says.

Read what Jeremiah Burroughs writes in his book, *The Rare Jewel of Christian Contentment*:

> Oh, Christian, if you have any faith, in the time of extremity think thus: this is the time that God calls for the exercise of faith. What can you do with your faith, if you cannot quiet your heart in discontent. There was a saying of one Dionysius, who had been a king, and afterwards was brought to such a low condition as to get his living by being a schoolmaster; someone comes and asks him, "what have you got by your philosophy from Plato and others?" "What have I got," he says, "I have got this, that though my condition is changed from so high a condition to low, yet I can be content." So what do you get by being a believer, a Christian? What can you do by your

faith? I can do this: I can in all states cast my care upon God, cast my burden upon God, I can commit my way to God in peace; Faith can do this. Therefore, when reason can go no higher, let faith get on the shoulders of reason and say, "I see land though reason cannot see it, I see good that will come out of all this evil."[52]

When we try to wander off from dwelling behind the veil, where God awaits in the secret place, when we rush out of the presence of fellowship with God because a trial has come, and we seek to go search for some tool or for some staff we can lean on to get us across this sudden flood, then we have actually run away from the source of all our guidance and protection. Instead, when the fires come raging in, we must stay behind the veil, dwelling in the secret place of the Most High and throwing all our cares and prayers and trust and hope upon the One who sits on the throne. If the fire ends up burning us to death, we know that we will be raised again before Him in whom we trust.

I once remarked to my friend during a trip where we barely caught our flight out of town that, "Life is a series of tight squeezes." I think I was actually hitting on something when I said that. When you are in that narrow cave of difficulty, instead of using up oxygen and panicking and running on ahead into passages you know nothing about, rather, you must learn to remain content. If God wills that we remain pinned between two boulders while we are in that "cave", we have faith that he will bring ravens from above to put food into our mouths and he will cause water to trickle down from the roof of the cavern in order to quench our thirst. We know that eventually, in His timing, He will come and get us out. We will not wander in the labyrinth forever. God will blow the roof off the thing one day and take us into glory. But all the while, Christ is with us in the darkness. He holds forth the lamp of His word to show us the path, and He knows what it is like to suffer in the dark places of the world.

---

[52] Jeremiah Burroughs. *The Rare Jewel of Christian Contentment.* (Banner of Truth Trust, 1964), 219

Christian, embrace the fact that God is going to keep sending you into the caverns, to teach you His ways and to teach you satisfaction in Him. This is the first step towards contentment. Seek to develop the skill to stay at the fountain's edge and to get all of your sustenance from God, the fountain of living waters. Stay behind the veil. Abide in Jesus. Feed upon the Bread of Life. Open your heart up to the Light of the World …. and the darkness in your mind will flee.

Have faith in the Son of God. Believe the power of Christ is at work in you, if indeed you are a Christian. Be confident He will finish what He started in you, and trust that He can give you growth in grace, because He rose from the dead.

"'Tis so sweet to trust in Jesus, Just to take him at his . Just to rest upon his promise. Just to know 'Thus saith the Lord'. Jesus, Jesus, how I trust him! How I've proved him o'er and o'er. Jesus, Jesus, precious Jesus. O for grace to trust him more!"

Contentment begins by beginning to rest and to be content with your current discontentment. It is being satisfied in Jesus, though you feel you are not being satisfied right now. And if you are abounding right now, it is remembering that you have been crucified with Christ, and that you are dead to sin, dead to the world, alive to God, and risen with Christ to walk in newness of life. We can do all things through Christ who strengthens us. Millions of Christians stand now before the throne of God, having been fully conformed into the image of Christ. The Spirit of God was able to bring them through life and teach them all in the school of Christ. Are we different from those who have gone before us in the faith? Are we so special, that Christ's resurrection power is unable to teach us how to be content? What will we believe? The lie? Or the Truth?

Conclusion

Living as a Christian in the midst of a wicked and perverse generation means that we must engage our warfare on the front line of battle. The front lines in this war for our souls is within the minds and hearts of God's people. The enemy will do whatever he can to water down our love and zeal for Christ and His ways.

The epistles of the New Testament drive home the indicatives of what Christ has accomplished for His people and the imperatives of how we are to respond to His love for us. Embedded within these great purposes of the apostolic writings are many themes and truths that relate to knowing the Lord and living for Him. We have seen in this book, that though the epistle to the Philippians is written with great general aims of rejoicing in Christ Jesus it also contains within it a minor theme of what the Christian's mind should be focusing on.

We have pulled out of different passages mental words that define the Philippians mindset: how the believer should think and what he should meditate on. We believe this mindset is essential for the Christian, especially in our day of constant distractions and the bombardment of information that constantly pelts against our brains. We cannot live for Christ if we do not pursue the mind of Christ.

And yet, all of this is extremely overwhelming to us. We all fall so short of being able to curb our wandering thoughts into focused meditation on the things of God the way we should. Who is sufficient to live as a Christian in the midst of this evil generation? We thank God, that it is through Christ alone that we can not only know forgiveness from our sins and shortcomings, but through our great Savior, can also know growth in holiness and godliness.

Paul ends his epistle to the Philippians by encouraging them and thanking them for the monetary gift they gave to him in his time of need. Though that is indeed the context, we end this book with the following words with the purpose of encouraging the Christian that God will indeed be faithful to cause us to be conformed into the image of Jesus Christ:

And my God shall supply all your need according to His riches in glory by Christ Jesus. Now to our God and Father be glory forever and ever. Amen.
-Philippians 4:19,20

Bibliography

Aland, Barbara, Kurt Aland, Johannes Karavidopoulos, Carlo M. Martini, and Bruce M. Metzger. *The UBS Greek New Testament Reader's Edition with Textual Notes.* Stuttgart: Deutsche Bibelgesellschaft, 2001.

Alexander, T. Desmond and Brian S. Rosner, eds. *New Dictionary of Biblical Theology.* Downers Groave: Inter-Varsity Press, 2000.

Brakel, Wilhelmus A. *The Christian's Reasonable Service, Vol. 4.* Grand Rapids: Reformation Heritage Books, 1995.

Brooks, Thomas. *Precious Remedies Against Satan's Devices.* Edinburgh: Banner of Truth Trust, 2011.

Burroughs, Jeremiah. *The Rare Jewel of Christian Contentment.* Edinburgh: Banner of Truth Trust, 1964.

Ellsworth, Roger. *Come Down, Lord!* Edinburgh: Banner of Truth Trust, 2009.

Ferguson, Sinclair B. *Let's Study Philippians.* Edinburgh: Banner of Truth Trust, 2010.

Hendriksen, William. *Galatians, Ephesians, Philippians, Colossians, and Philemon, New Testament Commentary.* Grand Rapids: Baker Academic, 1962.

Holy Bible, New King James Version. Nashville: Broadman & Holman Publishers, 1988.

Kittel, Gerhard and Gerhard Friedrich eds. *Theological Dictionary of the New Testament.* Grand Rapids: Wm. B. Eerdmans Publishing Company, 1964.

MacArthur, John. *The MacArthur New Testament Commentary, Philippians.* Chicago: Moody Press, 2001.

Murray, Iain. *D.M. Lloyd Jones, The Fight of Faith.* Edinburgh: The Banner of Truth Trust, 1990.

O'Brien, Peter T. *The Epistle to the Philippians, the New International Greek Testament Commentary.* Grand Rapids: Wm. B. Eerdmans Publishing Co., 1991.

Silva, Moses. *Philippians, Baker Exegetical Commentary on the New Testament.* Grand Rapids: Baker Academic, 2005.

Spurgeon, Charles. *An All-Round Ministry.* Pasadena: Pilgrim Publications, 1983.

Thayer, Joseph H. *Thayer's Greek-English Lexicon of the New Testament.* Grand Rapids: Hendrickson Publishers, 2014.

Trenchard, Warren C. *Complete Vocabulary Guide to the Greek New Testament Revised Edition.* Grand Rapids: Zondervan, 1998.

Watson, Thomas. *The Godly Man's Picture.* Edinburgh: Banner of Truth Trust, 2013.

www.ingramcontent.com/pod-product-compliance
Lightning Source LLC
Chambersburg PA
CBHW061326040426
42444CB00011B/2796